ANGLING *Life*

ANGLING *Life*

*A Fisherman Reflects on Success,
Failure, and the Ultimate Catch*

CAPTAIN DAN KEATING

TWO FISH PUBLISHING

Published by Two Fish Publishing
354 Sequoia Court
Antioch, Illinois 60002

Published in the United States of America

ISBN: 978-0-9774273-3-8

Interior design by Angie Messinger
Cover design by Josh Visser
Creative consultant: Mary Pudaite Keating

Set in Adobe Garamond.

To my son, Ethan Daniel.

You have an uncommon passion for life. Listen to your life.
Be strong and courageous as you discover the journey God
has set before you. Pursue it wisely and seek Him in all your ways.

Contents

Foreword

One recent Sunday morning just before the worship service started, my wife, Kathy, told me she had to go to the ladies' restroom with her best friend Patty. I thought it seemed a little junior high schoolish, a bit odd, but busied myself with adding the proper amount of cream, hot water and sugar into Kathy's coffee cup. But two minutes stretched to five, five minutes to 10, and I had to wonder what was up. Patty, a single mom in her mid-40s, whose only child, Ellery, is away at college, has battled multiple sclerosis while holding down a time-consuming job and struggling financially for several years. I thought she might have received some bad news about her health. Perhaps something bad had happened to Ellery. Maybe the bank was foreclosing on her home.

When both women came out of the bathroom dabbing at their eyes, I knew they couldn't have been discussing anything good and uplifting, but I was wrong—sort of. The congregation was singing and we had to find seats, so I didn't learn what they'd talked about until after the service.

"Patty told me that last week she decided to commit suicide," Kathy told me as I eased our truck out of the church parking lot. "She said she knew it would devastate Ellery, but that she would get over it. She was tired of always being in pain, of always having money problems. She was just going to drive her car really fast into a tree.

"She said she prayed about it and was sure that God didn't care. In fact, thinking about doing it gave her a sense of peace.

"But right after she made the decision, her mom called and told her that her great aunt had sent her a check, that she wanted Patty to have a thousand dollars. Just out of the blue."

Talk about a chilling, yet uplifting story! Thankfully, the funds were enough to ease some of Patty's burdens and she truly believes that the hidden hand of God was at work to dissuade her from ending her life.

Now, I grew up in a church-going family, but not long ago I would have pooh-poohed that hand of God stuff. The generosity of a great aunt coming out of the blue, just when Patty needed it most, was either damn good luck or a happy coincidence.

These days, as I grow in my own Christian faith, I truly believe it is God at work. It's the sort of miracle that I see more and more frequently and accept it as just that. God, supernaturally, fulfilling a need and helping his children believe. The event fills me with wonder, and affirms my own fledgling faith. It gives me confidence that not only does God exist, he's also watching out for us.

If there's a way to sum up *Angling Life: A Fisherman Reflects on Success, Failure, and the Ultimate Catch*, it's that author Captain Dan Keating, wants to show the reader how to attain a similar sense of wonder. Is this book religious? Sort of, but it's not really about religion. Is it about fishing? Definitely, but you're not going to find much "how-to" that will help catch more fish. What you will find, as you read, is the natural connection that anglers have to something bigger. The thing that helps explain why Jesus Christ signed commercial fishermen up to be part of his crew some 2,000 years ago. It's the thing that most fishermen know is there, but can't quite describe. The thing that leads us to the open waters of a stream, pond, lake or ocean where we put out lines and expect that soon, we'll be reeling in some fish.

In this book we meet the "old" Dan Keating, a young charter captain who used recreational drugs, was in constant conflict with conservation officers and who even shocked first-time fishing customers with his haircut. I have known the "new" Dan Keating for almost a decade now, and know him as a positive guy, a family man, a guy anyone would feel fortunate to call a friend. Most of what I know about Old Dan I learned as I edited this book. Sure, driving to fishing seminars we were presenting, or just shooting the breeze on the phone, New Dan gave me some glimpses of his former self. But in these pages, he really delves into his past as an up-and-coming charter captain. He shows how he was a self-reliant, cocky know-it-all, and reveals just how hugely unfulfilling and unsatisfactory his life was back then. He shows how his life changed so much for the better when he started finding the spirituality he so earnestly sought. Although his quest took him to such exotic, far-flung places as India, Nepal and the Maldives, he finally found the guide for his own life on the deck of his charter boat.

This is a fun book to read, as Captain Keating relates a lot of interesting experiences involving great storms and great catches, gleaned from a lifetime of fishing the huge, uncertain waters of Lake Michigan. He talks of fishing in primitive fashion aboard ancient looking boats in the Indian Ocean and South East Pacific and around his parents' home on Florida's Gulf Coast. I think that just about anyone who is interested in personal, spiritual growth will enjoy Dan's gentle narrative. And if you're a fisherman who occasionally marvels at how a piece of metal or wiggling plastic or a hand-tied hunk of feathers can catch a fish from the middle of nowhere, then you will enjoy reading—and learning from—this book most of all.

Dave Mull
Editor, *Great Lakes Angler Magazine*
Chicago, Illinois
November 2010

1

The Blue Horizon

I am haunted by water.

—Norman Maclean

A River Runs Through It

Maldivian fishermen are fearless. They venture out to sea day after day, guided solely by their instincts and yesterday's catch to fish deep, open water. Their boats are primitive at best. Their fishing method is well designed, yet simple—a hook and line.

Located in the middle of the Indian Ocean and surrounded by deep water, these islands are one of the world's largest fish magnets. Years ago, I was traveling in India and had the opportunity to visit these distant islands. For an American angler the Maldives are about as far off the beaten path as you can get. In fact, few Americans have seen this remote archipelago comprised of 26 atolls and 1,200 islands.

My adventure began in Malé, the capital of this island nation. Like any angler, I was irresistibly drawn to the city wharf. Late in the afternoon the wharf comes to life as a fleet of small wooden fishing boats (called dhonis) returns from the open ocean to unload their day's catch. What a sight! Tired looking wooden boats of 20- to 40-foot lengths jostle for a position at the wharf. Looking down into these vessels, I could not believe my eyes—fish were piled everywhere! I don't mean a cooler full of fish. I mean, the boats were literally stuffed full of fish . . . bow to stern, gunnel to gunnel—these boats were full of fish. It was an amazing sight, watching the men jump and scurry over piles of tuna and other assorted finned creatures lying on the decks, as they secured their boats to the dock and unloaded the day's catch. In all my fishing travels, I'd never seen such a sight.

After fishing all day under the hot, equatorial sun with hand lines and long wooden rods that resemble cane poles, Maldivian fishermen return late in the afternoon with boats full of tuna, dorado, wahoo, trevally, grouper, snapper and the occasional billfish. Day after day, I went down to the docks to watch these sun-drenched men unload their catches. Obviously the waters were teeming with fish—I *had* to get on the water! But how? There was no local charter fishing fleet. Plenty of dive boats, but all they wanted you to do was jump in the water and *look* at the fish. I wanted to do *battle* with the biggest, meanest fish I could find. The only option available was to go native and find a local fisherman who was willing to take a tourist sport fishing.

The hunt for a guide led me through the busy streets of Malé. After a number of communication failures and dead-end inquiries, I finally found our captain at the last place you would expect, a Muslim circumcision party. Mohammad Haleem was a local businessman and former politician who made his living catching live tropical fish on the reefs and exporting them to Singapore. He and I were from different worlds but when the conversation turned to fish, a bond instantly formed. He had no rods or reels, but he absolutely loved fish and fishing and passionately told me stories of a time he had taken some German tourists sport fishing. What Haleem lacked in equipment and experience he more than made up for with his enthusiasm and knowledge of the local waters. A simple handshake sealed our arrangement to venture out into the deep blue.

A few days later I met Haleem and his crew at the dock before sunrise. Haleem was a man of the sea. His lean frame, peppery-grey beard and sun-drenched skin, quickly conjured up images of The Old Man and the Sea. His weathered vessel, which had been painted green, sat expectantly at the dock. From all appearances, Haleem's 27-foot boat looked as if it had survived many skirmishes against the sea. Glancing into the boat I realized there were no rod holders, no radio, no electronics, and no steering wheel—just an open deck and a small housing covering the small diesel engine amidships. The fragile-looking wooden tiller hanging off the stern would guide our course through the heavy swells once we left the safety of the harbor.

Always the ready fisherman, I had dragged a wide selection of tackle halfway around the world. From small reef fish up to a mid-size marlin, I was prepared for battle. Unfortunately, the pre-dawn hours were not to the tired diesel engine's liking. Haleem and his nephew were charged up and ready for whatever the day would bring, but as I stowed the rods, reels and tackle on deck, the engine responded in a series of protesting gasps and grunts. Thirty-minutes later, I began to wonder if we would ever leave the dock. After much tinkering, the engine fired and we were off!

This was a real fishing trip! Other than the loud diesel engine and my tackle, there was not a sign of the 20th century anywhere on the boat. All we had to work with was Haleem's knowledge of the water, my limited supply of fishing gear, and an ancient looking boat. Once we cleared the protective barrier beyond Malé's harbor, the bottom fell away, straight down hundreds of feet into the mysterious depths. Haleem told me that the 200-fathom line was only minutes away. My excitement meter was red lining as Haleem steered the boat out to sea.

Blue. The horizon above, below and beyond was awash in an endless sea of blue. Only blue. And beneath my feet all that connected us to this endless sea was a tired, well-used wooden boat—that didn't seem altogether seaworthy. Would this be my last fishing trip? While we were completely alone and cut off from the modern world, I could not have been more alive.

When I take clients fishing on my charter boat, or even when I take her out by myself, I'm really not alone. I have a cell phone, marine radio, and the U.S. Coast Guard reasonably close for emergencies. I'm also in radio contact with other fishing captains. Here? We were pretty much on our own. There was not another boat in sight and we had no radio, no cell phone. If the engine failed or the boat sank, well, the outcome would certainly lead to a good story—if we survived. That said, the euphoria was heightened as the boat struggled against the massive swells rolling across the sea. In a timeless parade, these waves marched across the surface of the Indian Ocean, undaunted by our presence.

As the islands grew smaller astern and the primitive boat surged on, I realized how finite I was against the sea. Pondering my diminutive stature against the grand scheme of life, I unconsciously slipped the first lines into the water. A pair of 30-pound stand ups, held by two sets of hands, trailed the boat as we worked our way north, somewhere in the Indian Ocean. This was fishing as the Good Lord intended! Talk about not knowing what to expect . . . I didn't have a clue what we might catch nor did I have any idea what lay beneath the boat.

My mind may have been a million miles away but the sound of the reel's drag instantly brought me back. Something big and fast had crushed one of the orange and gold magnum Rapalas and tore off for the horizon. With line melting from the reel I got Haleem to stop the boat and we began fighting the strong fish. What would we pull from the sea? With great anticipation we finally saw the four-foot speedster appear below the boat, lit up in an array of iridescent blues and indigos—a wahoo. The fish was soon gaffed and after a brief photo session, the lines were quickly slipped back into the water. On this morning a steady bite of big wahoo and small tuna rescued me from my earlier ponderings.

I fished with Haleem for many days and we tangled with a wide variety of fish. From grouper to tuna to wahoo to billfish, the bite was exceptional. Haleem was enthralled. His love of the sound of a screaming drag as a large fish runs for the horizon, the feel of a rod under pressure and the challenge of the hunt was obvious. The passion and enthusiasm of fishing once again connected two people from very different backgrounds. As I departed the island, I knew that although we would never again meet, the memory of our time together would live on in the fishing equipment I left for my angling brother.

I returned from India and the Maldives in the spring of 1993 and went back to work on my third charter boat—a custom built 34-foot Atlantic Sportfisherman. Designed by a naval architect it was fast, sleek and boy, could it handle the waves! I could fish in heavy seas that forced most of my competition back to port. What a contrast my craft was to the *primitive* boats I fished on a few months earlier in the Maldives Islands.

My name is Dan Keating and I am a fortunate man, for I get paid to go fishing. Being a fishing guide requires me to wear many hats as I lead my clients to fish. I'm a counselor, referee, family therapist, bartender, business analyst, teacher, marketing guru, travel consultant, mechanic (not a very good one!) babysitter, janitor and friend—I'm a fishing guide. Before you tell me I'm the luckiest man alive, let me tell you; fishing for a living is hard work. Long hours, unpredictable weather (and customers!), equipment failure, fluctuating outcomes (both profit and catch) and long periods of extreme boredom punctuated by rapid adrenaline rushes define my world.

Sometimes, when the alarm clock goes off at 3:00 a.m. and thunder is ripping across the sky and my body aches from fishing in heavy seas for a week straight, I ask myself, *How did I end up with this life?* It's not like I woke up one morning and said, "I'm going to be a fishing guide!" It just sorta happened when my *hobby-out-of-control* got the best of me. When I was 18 I was a bit confused. (To be honest, I was really messed up!) I was unsure of what path to follow, so after starting college and discovering the *world*, I dropped out and started a charter fishing business on Lake Michigan. I always loved the water and fishing, and truth be told, I was pretty good at catching fish, so fishing and me were a perfect combination. As the River of Time swept me along in her shifting currents, fish became a big part of my life. Today, the most important relationships in my life (hi Honey, hi kids! I love ya!) are a reflection of my relationship to the water and my angling life.

Whether you are as crazy about fishing as I am, or just enjoy an occasional outing, you have to admit—our world is spinning faster than ever and before we know it, our lives are but a distant memory, sorta like yesterday's fishing trip. Fishing takes us beyond the murky waters; beyond the noise and clutter of our busy lives and helps us to gain perspective on life and what matters most. When we grab our favorite rod and head down to a pond, stream, lake or seashore, nature itself breathes life into our soul as it connects us to something far greater than ourselves. From first light, to the distant echo of the loon to the roar of the wind across the water, there's something deep and compelling about the outdoors that calls out to us, that beckons us to come closer, and that speaks profound truth into the meaning of our lives.

In the pages ahead I want to explore our angling passion and its connection to life. Life, and a day on the water, are both filled with risk and the promise of great rewards. In his book *Wild at Heart*, John Eldridge writes that a man's heart is designed for adventure and that we long for excitement. I think that's why we like fishing so much! Just like life, a good day on the water is often filled with challenges; some small and some rather profound, like Joe's battle with a marlin and a broken reel (which you can read about in chapter 8). There's also a bit of mystery in angling and life, as each requires degrees of faith. Before I ever untie my boat from the dock, I look across the water and while I don't *see* the fish, I have faith that I will catch them. Once on the water we place our faith in our equipment, our boats and motors and even in our favorite fishing spots. Life is also filled with unseen realities and it takes a lot of faith to navigate the landscape of time, relationships, technology, work and leisure.

As we journey together I also want to introduce you to an ancient fisherman—Simon Peter. I met him in the pages of the Bible and even though he lived many years ago we share a common bond. Like us, he longed for adventure, struggled through *boatloads of challenges* and was thrilled with a great catch of fish.

So come on a journey with me! We'll talk about life, meet some ancient fishermen and tell some fishing yarns along the way. As your guide through these pages I want you to understand that even after all my years on the water, I'm still excited by every strike and the many challenges encountered when fishing. No matter how many fish we catch, fishing can fill our soul with a sense of hope and an anticipation of what might happen when we launch our boats and commence a safari into deep waters. Let's begin our journey together by taking a closer look at what keeps calling us back to the angling life.

The sea has never been friendly to man.
At most it has been the accomplice
of human restlessness.
—JOSEPH CONRAD

2

Why Fish?

*Many go fishing all their lives without
knowing it is not fish they are after.*
—HENRY DAVID THOREAU

Gulf Coast passes are always exciting places to fish. Tides flow through coastal passes magically transforming them into fish highways that attract a wide variety of sea creatures. From sharks, dolphins and stingrays, to vast schools of ladyfish, succulent pompano, blue fish, massive cobia, trout, jacks, mackerel, snook, reds, tarpon, snapper, sheepshead, and grouper, the list goes on, and you never know what you'll catch—until you start fishing.

One winter day a few years ago, my family and I were fishing together on Sarasota's Big Pass. On this day the tide was flowing out strongly. Everywhere you looked, gulls wheeled overhead, telling us the pass was full of bait and game fish. I knew we were going to catch fish. As I scanned the surface for signs of life, my gut told me it would only be a matter of time before the day's cast of characters showed up for the afternoon feed.

I shut the engine off midway through the pass so we could drift with the falling tide along the flats edging the deep channel. My wife, Mary, and our three oldest children were ready to fish. Let me warn you, what ensued was a bit chaotic, but could this crew ever catch fish! Our oldest daughter, Rebecca, all of seven years old, was first to fire a cast from the bow into the aqua green water flowing out of Sarasota Bay. I set up four-year-old Ethan with a live shrimp in the stern and helped him cast, placing the rod in a rod holder and telling him to watch the line closely. Mary, wearing our 22-pound Kate in a baby harness, got into the act when she launched her first cast and before I could pick up my own rod, screams of excitement came from the bow. Rebecca was hooked up with a hard charging fish that was trying to wrench the rod from her second-grader hands. Suddenly, Ethan's line took off and before I could convince Ethan to take his rod out of the rod holder, Mary's line was hit! A triple-header—and our lines had only just gotten wet!

For the next half hour it was pure and joyous pandemonium. Mary and the kids were hooked up constantly with ladyfish, blue fish, mackerel and pompano. As the fish catching-frenzy continued, a local guide quietly pulled up to our location from the east. What do you suppose was going through his mind as he watched this middle-aged father frantically doing laps around the side-console 19-foot boat, trying to unhook fish, untangle lines and bait hooks? Between the fish flying out of the water and screaming kids, I bet he thought he hit the jackpot!

This guide did what any one of us voracious anglers would do. He motored up current a respectable distance and began drifting through the same stretch of water. A falling tide turns Big Pass into a river and anglers must control the speed of their boats' drift if they want to catch fish. His three enthusiastic clients began beating the water vigorously. Cast, after cast, after cast, they kept at it. But something was wrong.

Pause for a moment and try to picture this scene. Two boats drifting the same path, less than 100 yards apart. On one boat, confusion and excitement reigned: fish flying out of the water, lines breaking, lures sailing through the air, fish being released—and children bursting with laughter!

On the other boat? Three fishless men, growing more aggravated with each fish released across the way. They continued to flail the water yet their hooks returned fishless every time. I could feel their frustration from our boat. I couldn't help but wonder why the guide kept his clients so close to us for so long. I've been a guide for over 25 years and it is humiliating to have your lunch handed to you by a recreational angler, let alone a bunch of half pints with Mom and Dad.

What was this guide thinking? It was obvious that tons of fish were in the area. His clients changed lures, lines, colors, and retrieves, yet, cast after cast, they failed to hook up. And to add insult to injury, only a short distance across the water the kids were absolutely beating on the fish.

Why were these anglers having so much trouble catching fish? They were fishing nearly on top of us but they failed to notice one small, yet very important detail. The fish in this particular school were in a negative mood, holding tight to the bottom. My children were fishing live bait slow, dragging tasty, live shrimp right under the fish's noses. The enthusiastic clients were fishing their artificial lures too high and too fast.

Eventually the guide (who never figured out what we were doing differently) and his clients got tired of watching us catch fish and they took off for bluer waters. My family, however, spent the rest of the afternoon in Big Pass enjoying each other's company, the beauty of the ocean, while laughing the whole time. And yes, we caught and released loads of fish. Even though I make my living leading others to fish, I still love fishing, even on my vacations.

I don't think I'm the only person like this. According to government statistics, roughly 30 million adults buy a fishing license in the United States every year. If you could look into the garages and crawl spaces of America, few would be the homes where hooks, line and sinker were absent. It is undeniable—the joy of fishing is a part of many people's lives.

Those who have not been infected by the bug don't understand what makes our pulse quicken as we walk the aisles of our favorite tackle store, peruse the latest catalog, or browse the latest online selection of new tackle. They don't understand why we would subject our bodies to the beating of heavy seas or why we would stand in a cold rain for hours, waiting patiently, hoping for a bite. Most likely, they do not understand the thrill that sends us into overdrive as we feel the pull of an unseen adversary on the end of our line. Be it a 9-inch sunfish, a 10-pound bass or a 200-pound marlin, fishing connects us to a sense of mystery.

Why do we go fishing? Is it visions of fish crackling in hot oil and the sweet taste of fresh filets that you didn't buy at the grocery store? Is it the thrill of the hunt or the anticipation of the strike? A true fisherman always expects one more strike. Musky anglers know this feeling all too well. No matter how slow the day, no matter how high the odds are stacked against him, a fisherman believes there will always be one more cast . . . one more strike . . . one more fish to catch . . . one more adventure to live.

But maybe, just maybe, our love of fishing is more complex than fish and water alone. What is it about fishing that draws you back to the water? Henry David Thoreau once said, "Many go fishing all their lives without knowing it is not fish they are after." When you float down a river, do you take the time to explore eddies and quiet pools in search of trophies? You may even beach the boat to explore more thoroughly a hidden pool. Some of life's most treasured memories are found far from the beaten path. Like us as we drift downstream on the river of time, the current seems to quicken as we get older. Is a fishing trip that much different than life?

When you were young, time seemed to stretch endlessly to the horizon. As a child, each new day was an adventure. You took the time to turn over rocks and investigate the creatures that squirmed in the soil.

You were never in a hurry as you walked home from school. But as an adult time has become a precious commodity that you never seem to have enough of. Tournament anglers who come to the weigh-ins one or two fish short of a limit sometimes say they just ran out of time. As you age, time can become an enemy, as the days seem to grow shorter and pass by more quickly.

The pace of modern life is frighteningly fast and if you are not careful, the current will sweep you past life's hidden treasures. Fishing connects us to life. It is one of those rare, multi-dimensional activities that allows you time to think and to build lasting relationships with people and with place.

The fabric of our very existence is woven through these relationships and if you reflect on your love of fishing, you may find that a combination of these relationships and experiences have nurtured your angling passion.

My own love for the sport began this way. My father patiently spent Saturday mornings with me on a 17-foot Boston Whaler, the *Frick 'N Frack,* trolling the cold waters of Lake Michigan for salmon and trout. My mother sacrificed time to take me ice fishing during the dark of winter. Two grandfathers explored riverbanks and shared their fishing secrets with me, a wide-eyed youth. A local pond was my constant companion that magically soothed my adolescent emotions, day after day. A campsite on the shores of Basswood Lake planted the seeds of adventure in my heart.

One location that had a particularly profound impact on my love for open water was Wrightsville Beach, North Carolina, where we went on a family vacation. I can still taste the salty sea air and smell rotting shrimp as I think of my father walking me down the pier. The sound of the breakers crashing against the pilings echoes through my mind.

From a seven-year-old's perspective, the pier seemed to stretch halfway across the Atlantic. Anticipation flooded my spirit that day as I sat on the pier waiting for a bluefish to take my bait and accept the challenge of a dreamy boy. That particular fight never materialized, but that pier led me a few steps closer to my angling destiny.

You see, it was at Wrightsville Beach where my dad graduated me from the pier to the mysterious world of deep-sea fishing. Sleep did not come easy the night before we embarked on that first voyage. My mind refused to let sleep intrude as thoughts of giant billfish and other exotic trophies flooded my imagination. Yet, my expectations of that first trip offshore were quite different from the reality of that day. A storm system known as Hurricane Agnes had passed through the region, leaving a heavy swell in her wake.

We boarded the large, steel-hulled behemoth early the next morning. After clearing the inlet, the big diesels growled as we battled the heavy swells on our way to the deep, offshore waters, and I was quickly introduced to the humbling experience of seasickness. My dad and I never made it on deck to wet a line, yet dad and I forged a unique bond as he stayed by the side of an enthusiastic little boy who could do nothing more than vomit between tears, too sick to put a line in the water. We may have walked off that boat without a single fish, but the sea, and the sense of adventure that accompanies any trip into deep water, captured my heart and drew me closer to my destiny as a big water sport fishing captain.

What do the pages of your life story reflect? Do the memories of yesterday's fishing adventures connect you to friends, family and the landscape? Or, is there a deeper, almost mystical current pulling at your soul? What draws us to the water and the anticipation of one more cast, one more strike, one more trophy to catch, one more adventure to live?

If you want to make a sweet memory
With your kids, here's the recipe
Peanut butter and a jar of jam
Loaf of bread and pop in a can
Bamboo poles and hooks on the line
Can of worms and some of your time
And don't forget that little round bobber
Then all you do is, just add water
Just add water
Don't have to be deep
Take'em to the banks of a big lake
Or a little creek
Sweet memories with your sons and your daughters
That's what you'll get
When you just add water
You can take your phone but leave it off
Turn on your heart and let it talk
Cause words come easy, when you're fishin'
And when they talk make sure you listen
And if the weather turns hot
And the fish go hide
Don't pack it up and run back inside
Just tell your kids, "do like your father"
Roll up your pants, and just add water
—STEVE CHAPMAN
"Just Add Water"

3

The Heart of a Fisherman

*When it comes to the future, our lives
are more discovered than determined.*
—Erwin Raphael McManus
Wide Awake

My nine-year-old son Ethan does everything with gusto; from the moment he wakes and his feet hit the ground running to the moment he lays his head on the pillow and drifts off to sleep. Playing with LEGO blocks, defeating the Evil Empire in the back yard or studying for a spelling test, he knows one speed—*da-da-da-dat da-da*—charge!

Do you remember what it was like to be nine years old? Your imagination was limitless and time seemed to stretch beyond the horizon. The dreams of a young boy are as big as the Western landscape. *Where will my journey take me? What will I accomplish? Will I capture the princess and live in the castle?* Fast-forward a few years to the present. Do your feet hit the floor each morning with anticipation? Do you pursue life with passion? Or, has a fog bank obscured the horizon and burdened your steps?

I've come to realize that life and fishing are deeply connected. In *Wide Awake*, Erwin Raphael McManus says, "When it comes to the future, our lives are more discovered than determined." Your life and every day on the water are a journey of discovery. Before the first cast hits the water, you have an internal sense of anticipation of what might be. A sense of mystery pervades. What will I catch? How many? How big? Will the lake be gracious to me, or will it test my stamina and will?

Some days will present us with clear skies, calm seas and fish on almost every cast. Other days, however, will be filled with storm clouds, tangled lines, and empty casts. You may drive for hours in the predawn darkness only to find angry seas pounding on the breakwalls. After planning a vacation for months you may arrive at your destination only to be greeted by torrential rains or an outboard motor that refuses to start. Then, there are the fish—they don't always follow the rules. You may finally hook the fish you've been searching for, only to have your line break with the prize inches from the net.

Just like the angry seas and a lost fish, the circumstances and relationships of life don't always meet our expectations. Dreams go unanswered, people disappoint us and our health continues to decay. But no matter what life brings you, retreating to the outdoors and spending a day on the water restores your spirits and strengthens your heart. The magnetic draw of fishing frequently begins early in life and is nurtured by sunrises, summer storms, conquered adversity, photographs of trophy fish and tales of yesterday's adventures and tomorrow's dreams. For many, it becomes an obsession. Like an appetite, it is powerful, and if given the chance, it can consume you. For all of us anglers, though, our enthusiasm finds its deepest expression and fulfillment when we're on the water.

Where does this magnetic, almost magical attraction to water and the great outdoors come from? Looking back to the headwaters of my angling heart, it is quite apparent that I was drawn to water like a little boy is drawn to puddles. When I was a young child, my family would make a trip each summer to central Iowa. To a six-year-old boy the fields and rivers of central Iowa were Disney World and the Garden of Eden rolled into one great play land!

These journeys really began before we ever crossed the Mississippi River. My family would load the car with luggage, snacks and dreams of what the week ahead would hold. Cruising west down Highway 80, my two sisters and I would arrange ourselves around the car (no seat belt laws!) and fall asleep to the hum of the motor, static AM radio and dreams of Gam's hot fudge sundaes. My grandma had a sweet tooth and always loaded her sundaes with gobs of hot fudge, whipped cream and loads of plump cashews.

Once we arrived in Des Moines, our horizons were greatly expanded. Young boys full of energy and imagination don't just go fishing, they *go on adventures*. Do you remember what it was like to be six years old? The imagination of a young boy is as vast as the seven seas and as creative as a first-grade classroom. My early Hawkeye fishing trips were true adventures that typically began the night before. You see, Granddad believed the best fishing bait was a fat, juicy night crawler. Growing up, you didn't go to a vending machine to buy bait. The best worm was a worm you pulled from the earth with your own hand after a hard rain. So with flashlights in hand we scoured the lawn for tomorrow's bait.

We would awaken the following morning to the rich aroma of Gam's rib-sticking bacon and egg breakfast. After the morning feast my sisters, cousins and I would pack into Granddad's car and drive down to the Skunk, Raccoon or Des Moines rivers. Our expectations were set on giant flathead catfish, but anything with fins—from tiny sunfish to bullheads to channel cats or carp (the golden queen of the river)—would satisfy our youthful fascination to know what was lurking beneath the surface of those muddy rivers. Truth be told, we never caught many fish on those rivers, but those early fishing trips firmly planted the spirit of adventure in my heart.

Perhaps you were drawn to fishing at an early age. Maybe it was the first sight of a bobber dipping beneath the surface. Maybe it was that muggy summer afternoon, toes dangling in the water, when an unknown tug on the end of the line pulled you out of a dream. But at one time, on some river, lake or ocean, something happened. Deep within your heart, something was triggered. Fishing was in your blood for life. Fishing, and the events surrounding fishing, pierced your soul.

For many, angling is more than just the act of putting a line in the water. For a young child, looking for worms on a warm summer night or exploring the edge of a streambed is as entertaining as the fishing itself. For an adult the journey to a favorite destination, or overcoming adversity against nature and building relationships with friends, are often as memorable as the catch. Rigging tackle the night before is almost as fun as reeling in a fish.

For some of us, the need to wet a line feels almost as important as breathing. Lack of oxygen leads to death but fishing leads us to life. While not as extreme as the body's need for oxygen, the need to nourish the soul is vital. Maybe that's why we're so passionate about fishing; because it connects us to something bigger than ourselves. From the anticipation, to the preparation, to the journey, to the catch, and home again, the world surrounding fishing nurtures our souls; and waters our lives with beauty, refreshment, challenge, mystery, fellowship and rewards.

Once the love of fishing gets hold of you, there is no escaping its mystical tug on your soul. No matter how busy you become, you still have that internal pull that captivates your imagination and quickens your pulse as you approach the water. Fishing, and the emotions it generates, become a part of you. Whether you live in a desert or along the water's edge, you cannot escape the magnetic draw.

Yes, the love of fishing is a passion that resonates deep within one's heart. If you understand this thought, then take a moment to ponder the question of passion. Why do you love fishing and the outdoors so much? *Where* does your passion come from? Is it a gift from beyond you?

A gift involves two persons—the giver and the recipient. If passion is a gift, then who gave it to you? Could it be that your love of the water is a gift from the one who created the water, the sky and everything else we enjoy about nature?

I remember a time in my life when this thought was absurd! But I couldn't escape the thought, *What if God is real?* Did God create the woods and waters I loved? Did God plant a desire to enjoy nature deep in my heart? Did God breathe the gift of passion into my soul when he formed me?

On a recent family trip to Florida, Ethan was more excited about fishing than I'd ever seen him. Whether we were going offshore in pursuit of kingfish, mackerel, and tuna or into the backcountry to chase snook and anything else with fins, he wanted to be a part of the action! Where does Ethan's enthusiasm come from? Is passion simply a physical thing, a memory or the adrenaline rush and anticipation of another adventure? Or, is passion deeper than the waters we fish? Ethan's natural, inborn enthusiasm for living seems as much a God-given gift as the waters, the sunrise and the freedom to be out pursuing the passion.

In the midst of your journey, escape to a quiet moment and ponder the thought of passion. Ask yourself: Is it possible that God designed you to enjoy the outdoors? If this is at all possible, what kind of God is he? Is he like a distant watchmaker, who created this complex world and then just wound it up and left? Or is he the kind of God who takes a deep interest in what happens here, and even a deep interest in you?

Even if you don't buy the Creator angle (and there was a time when I didn't), we can learn a lot by asking, "Why am I so passionate about fishing?" Let's pursue this thought together. Let's ponder the thought of God and passion, and enjoy a few fishing experiences in the process.

> *The older we get the more we need somebody*
> *bigger than we are to restore what we have lost.*
> *Deep within every human heart throbs the undying hope*
> *that somebody or something will bring both an explanation*
> *of what life is all about and a way to retain the wonder. Yet*
> *if we would but pause and first ponder what it is that we*
> *already see in this world of wonder we might get a brief taste*
> *of the wonder that may be poured into us as well.*
>
> —RAVI ZACHARIAS
> *Recapture the Wonder*

4

The Fingerprints of God

When one tugs on a single thing in nature,
one finds it attached to the rest of the world.
—JOHN MUIR

I love running offshore to deep blue water in pursuit of trophy king salmon and steelhead. These deepwater brutes are sometimes as long as your leg and they practically rip the rod out of the rod holder when they strike. When you hook one of these gladiators they often leap repeatedly from the water and make sizzling runs that will test your arms and your tackle. But I need to make a confession. You see, until life's journey transplanted me to the front range of the Colorado Rockies for two years, I had become a bit of a snob, actually thinking less of some anglers; particularly those who like to fly fish for inland trout in mountain lakes and streams.

Have you ever been to the Colorado Front Range? After studying a map I quickly realized I was in trouble—there was not much water out there! Large or small, water is a precious commodity out west, and people have been fighting over it for years. How could a man live in such a location? After all, I was raised on big water and big fish. I was accustomed to hearing the sound of a reel's drag as a salmon ran toward the horizon. Where would I go fishing in the midst of all those rocks and mountains? Would I ever hear the sound of a singing reel again? I thought I might wither up and fade like my prospects for fishing.

Guess what? I discovered that some of the bluest, cleanest water in the world is found above 10,000 feet. Thanks to my friends Bruce and Chuck, I also learned that the mountains were full of treasure—and the treasure had fins! I discovered that for those who were not afraid to wander from the beaten path, adventure awaited. I soon realized that a rigorous hike made the fishing even more rewarding. I fell in love with fishing all over again. Maybe, surrounded by all that rock, I gained a deeper appreciation of water.

Walk with me for a moment. Unleash your imagination, grab your fly rod (or an ultra-light spinning rod), a backpack and put yourself on the side of a mountain. Let's journey together into the high terrain of the great outdoors.

The trail starts out easy enough, but as you wind your way up the side of the mountain your breathing reflects the increased angle of the trail. The trail narrows as you ascend farther into the dense stand of aspen and towering pines. Massive boulders strewn along the path lead you to speculate about the events that shook their giant bulk free from the earth.

Working your way up the trail, the brilliance and vastness of the sky overwhelms you and magnifies the immensities of the land below. The dropping air temperature invigorates your mind and body. Take a moment, catch your breath and ponder the breathtaking beauty of the rugged landscape around you. Climbing higher into the unknown, visions of dancing trout fill your imagination.

As you round a bend in the trail, an opening in the thick aspen veil gives you a view across the valley—you are captivated by the vista that confronts you. The jagged edges of the horizon tear at your soul. How long, you wonder, would it take to scale their heights? Could you reach their snow-capped summits? Could you touch heaven?

With a seemingly endless blue sky above and the rocky trail beneath your feet you feel as if you are straddling a boundary, caught between two conflicting worlds. This perilous frontier between sky and mountain beckons the pilgrim upward to explore her hidden mysteries. The beauty of this unforgiving world feeds your spirit and leads you to forget yourself and the struggles of life as you drink in the grandeur of creation.

Continuing up the trail, your feet cross the tracks of a cougar. There is no mistaking the marks of this beast—the big cat's front paws leave a larger imprint in the earth than the hind paws. For just a moment, you follow the cat's path and notice that he is tracking a deer. Life, in all its mystery, goes on.

The trail rounds yet another bend, which takes you dangerously close to the canyon rim. The rocky edge falls away hundreds of feet, straight down, only to be caught in a blanket of blue spruce pines. Sharp edges of the unforgiving landscape remind you of your frail mortality. As your heart rate quickens, you realize one slight misstep on the narrow trail and your life and limbs would be shattered against the rocks below.

The higher you climb, the sparser life becomes. Yet seemingly out of nowhere, a mountain stream cascades down its timeless path, washing over ancient rocks perfectly inserted into the streambed by an artist's hand. You break away from the trail and follow the stream down a ravine. Where will this life-giving artery lead you? Anticipation builds as you descend into the valley. You round yet another bend and the dense canopy of aspens and pines gives way to a clearing. You are flooded with light as you catch the first glimpse of the small mountain lake nestled gently in this high-altitude valley. With the mountains rising above, there, at your feet, like a jewel perfectly inserted into a king's crown, lies the most pristine lake imaginable.

Your heart pumps faster as you see signs of life upon the calm surface of this cerulean gem. The surface of the lake is dimpled with the ringlets made by feeding cutthroats and rainbows. In a timeless dance, the trout rise to the surface to gently inhale the day's feast of caddis and stoneflies. How odd, in such a cruel environment, these tiny insects with a lifespan of only a few hours sustain these magnificent trout. As you reflect on the landscape and the beauty you saw hiking up the trail, pause for a moment and ponder the question of creation. Who raised the mountains from the earth below? Who carved the canyons and paints the sky all the shades of a rainbow day after day? Who filled the night sky with endless lights? Who gives the eagle flight? Who painted the spots on the brook trout? Who gave the bull elk its voice? When I stand outdoors and soak it all in, the vastness, the mystery, the magnificence of it all, my heart is flooded with amazement and wonder: Where does it all come from?

An ancient king once looked across the horizon and was moved to declare, *He set the earth on its foundations . . . the mountains rose, the valleys sank down to the place that you appointed for them* (Psalm 104:5,8).

The Puzzle of Life

My daughter Kate has always loved puzzles! After enthusiastically opening the box, she dumps hundreds of pieces on the table, some spilling to the floor. She looks at the scattered pieces and wonders how this will amount to anything, yet she knows the potential of the finished product. When a puzzle is fully assembled the pieces all fit together to form a complete picture. Each piece has its exact purpose and place in the whole.

If you have spent anytime outdoors, you have to admit, nature is amazing. Step outside and examine a handful of dirt, as six-year-old Kate and her younger sister Chloë did one fall day. It was a bright

November afternoon and they wanted to help dad weed the garden. So, with shovels in hand and bare feet covered in dirt, the two girls dug into the ground and discovered a world full of life beneath the surface. Worms, slugs and a host of other living creatures were soon given names as the girls wondered how these creatures buried in the ground could see and poop. Oh, to be young again!

Life comes in a staggering variety of forms we never think about. Put a handful of that dirt under an electron microscope and you discover that countless microorganisms thrive there. The complexity of their cell structure and purpose is not fully understood by the scientific community, yet they exist beneath our feet, just as Kate and Chloë discovered.

So maybe you haven't dug in the dirt lately, but have you ever looked up at the night sky and pondered how far up it goes? When I moved to Colorado, my buddy Bruce took me for a July fishing and camping trip. The fishing, hiking and companionship were great, even though Bruce failed to tell me just how cold the mountains could get at night. But, late at night after the campfire was extinguished, far, far away from the glow of city lights, I looked up into the blackest sky imaginable. What I saw was amazing—an endless sea of stars was splashed across the night canvas. Do they go on forever?

Whether you look at the universe through the lens of a microscope, a telescope, or your own eyes, this world is amazingly complex. A multitude of species and ecosystems fit together in an intricate dance of interlocking dependency. From the finely tuned gravity fields found within all sub-atomic structures to the intricacies of the human DNA sequence to the oceanic currents that drive continental weather patterns to the perfect balance that holds the solar system together—life, is truly amazing!

But within the complexity, there is order and purpose. From the ebb and flow of the tides to the rhythm of the four seasons that renew the landscape with life each spring, life flows through the layers of the world in a seamless connection. Think of fish—why in the world does a carp feed on the bottom of a lake? Who taught a trout to feed on the surface? How did a creature as massive as a whale shark ever figure out he was to eat the smallest of creatures—plankton? Is this world and all its complexities a cosmic accident? Or is a living, intelligent designer responsible? Could there be a grand scheme to this madness we call life?

Leading scientists theorize that a random explosion deep in the recesses of time ignited a flow of motion and matter that, by chance, happened to form a rock we call earth. This rock, again by chance, happened to end up in just the right location, balanced perfectly between the sun and the other solar systems. A few thousand miles closer or farther from the sun, and the environment would be too hostile to support life. And, wouldn't you know it, an atmosphere, gravity and all the laws of physics we take for granted just came into being, and—voila!—it all held together! And mysteriously, water appeared and somehow, a single-celled organism emerged from the soup and then, somehow, it became more and more complex and before you know it, you and I emerged from a swamp, and now, here we are, at the end of an evolutionary journey, sitting comfortably at the top of the food chain! Let me ask you, could this magnificent puzzle really have assembled itself?

Like the pieces of a puzzle scattered across a table, the individual components of life (big and small) don't look like much when viewed alone. It is only when they are connected that life happens. The separate pieces form a complete picture through a complex series of relationships that define and sustain them. From single-celled organisms to complete ecosystems life in all its mystery and intricacy interlocks like a puzzle. Just like a puzzle, when life's individual pieces are properly assembled, the world is complete. As John Muir eloquently stated, "When one tugs on a single thing in nature, one finds it attached to the rest of the world."

The woods and waters of this world call out to you. They beckon you to look beyond yourself. For just a moment, ponder the thought of creation. Ask yourself, "Where did it all come from?" Are the mountains, plants, trees, birds, fish and animals an accident? Are the sunsets and summer thunderstorms that give texture to our world a cosmic coincidence? Are the family members and friends that you enjoy spending time with the product of billions and billions of random mutations? Or did an intelligent being, a creator, reach out from the shores of eternity and bring this world into existence?

Did he create the world in a chaotic fashion, much like a child taking an assortment of paint bottles and spilling them on a canvas? Or did he meticulously and intelligently apply one color at a time, blending them into a complete picture?

I used to have a very limited understanding of God. For much of my life I thought God was a prisoner held captive in dusty old churches, a being who would rarely venture forth from sacred writings to mingle with the created world. But the more time I spent outdoors, the more I began to see his fingerprints, his brushstrokes scattered across the canvas of creation. From the starry sky above, to the wings of the dawn, to the mysterious depths of the sea, God's fingerprints are unmistakable—he is an artist!

Artists reveal themselves through their creative work. What kind of artist would create a crystalline mountain stream, place it in a perfect setting above 10,000 feet, then splash the stream through a rugged canyon and fill the water with fish more beautiful than a 17th century Rembrandt painting? I believe God created the natural world. The opening verses of the Bible tell us, "In the beginning, God created the heavens and the earth," and I believe that he is the eternal architect who made the rocks, streams and fish! That ancient king I mentioned above? He too was moved by the beauty of water, writing, "O Lord, . . . the earth is full of your creatures. Here is the sea, great and wide, which teems with creatures innumerable, living things both small and great . . . These all look to you to give them their food in due season. When you give it to them, they gather it up" (King David, Psalm 104).

If an intelligent being is responsible for creating the lakes, rivers, mountains and the creatures that inhabit them, then is it possible that he uniquely created you? Are you just another late model, assembly line production of *homo sapiens*, or are you a one of a kind, limited edition model that was designed with a purpose in mind? Is there a deeper meaning to life than just paying bills and amassing more stuff?

I'm convinced that there is, and that it is connected to our passion for fishing. Why do we feel so alive when we are outdoors? As the Irish Poet Van Morrison sang in his hit song "And It Stoned Me," why do we enjoy standing outside, "as the rain keep pourin' down . . . hands are full of a fishin' rod, and the tackle on our backs?" Why do we spend countless hours dangling hooks and lures in the water, hoping to catch a fish? Why does the sight of the mountains at sunset take our breath away? It's almost like our love of the outdoors is hardwired into our DNA! But think about it. If God is an artist who expresses himself through his creation, then you (his creation) are an expression of God. It says in the Bible (right in the very first chapter) "God created man in his own image, in the image of God he created him; male and female" (Genesis 1:27).

If God is responsible for creation and the passion that breathes life into our soul is it possible that he wants to reveal more of himself to us? Let's explore what it might have been like to go fishing in the days of old. An ancient fisherman who made his living on a treacherous lake may lead us to a deeper understanding of God, and ourselves, along the way.

> *For His invisible attributes, namely, His eternal power and*
> *divine nature, have been clearly perceived, ever since the*
> *creation of the world, in the things that have been made.*
> —ROMANS 1:20

> *By and large, our world has lost its sense of wonder. We*
> *have grown up. We no longer catch our breath at the sight*
> *of a rainbow or the scent of a rose, as we once did. We have*
> *grown bigger and everything else smaller, less impressive.*
> *We no longer run our fingers through water, no longer*
> *shout at the stars or make faces at the moon. Water is H_2O,*
> *the stars have been classified, and the moon is not made of*
> *green cheese. Thanks to satellite, TV and jet*
> *planes we can visit places available in the past only to*
> *Columbus, a Balboa and other daring explorers.*
> —BRENNAN MANNING
> *The Ragamuffin Gospel*

5

My Honeymoon Barracuda

When you fish for love,
bait with your heart, not your brain.
—MARK TWAIN

My life has been one long fishing trip, so it was only fitting that my new wife and I went fishing on our honeymoon. Mary had saved her airline miles from years of travel-related work so we could have a real, first class honeymoon in Bali, an island in Indonesia. It could not have been better. The weather was wonderful and the destination exotic. From the first-class seats on the airline, to the luxury hotel and exquisite food, everything was first class . . . until we went fishing.

While Bali is a popular travel destination, it is not well known for its angling opportunities. That, however, was not a big problem for a fishing guide like me, who drags rods, reels, lures and terminal tackle everywhere he goes and thinks he can catch fish wherever water is found.

In Bali we did the normal touristy stuff all honeymoon couples do, but we also investigated the local fishing scene. It quickly became apparent that our sport fishing options were rather limited. Eventually we located an Australian captain who had a fairly modern sport fishing boat. Based on his photos of tuna, billfish and wahoo, it looked like he caught fish. But then I saw his rates—ouch, he was expensive! But, if the guy could put us on fish, money was no object, so I proceeded to ask my list of questions. After talking with the captain for a few minutes my internal warning alarm started whooping. When you make a career out of fishing, you learn how to read between the lines. This guy's complete lack of enthusiasm over our chances of catching fish led me to believe that he offered little more than a very expensive boat ride. But we still wanted to go fishing so we continued to hunt for another option and eventually found a local tour operator who offered fishing trips on traditional Indonesian fishing boats. What is a *traditional Indonesian* fishing boat? From a distance, it looks like a giant canoe your grandfather might have bought at a rummage sale. As you get closer, you begin to wonder if it is a relic that archeologists unearthed from Neptune's vault. It's made of wood, wood that looks really old and has survived many battles with the sea. Outriggers attached to each side aren't for running lines, but to keep the boat from rolling over in the waves. In other words, the boat was perfect for a honeymoon adventure and we booked our outing for the following day.

We arose early in the morning, and after a short cab ride we arrived at the coast. The boat was beached and looked as if it were waiting for us. As we waded into the surf and climbed over the low gunnel, I felt as if we were stepping back in time. Other than the rods, reels and a handful of lures I was carrying, we were pretty much leaving the modern world behind. The boat had no electronics, only a small outboard motor, some fuel (hopefully enough to return) and a pair of rod holders. What more did we need?

Once onboard, I quickly discovered that our guide did not speak much English. No problem, I didn't speak much Balinese but we were both fisherman and we both wanted to catch fish. Somehow, in that universal language common to all anglers, we would get along just fine. We motored out of the protective cove and beyond the reefs and soon found ourselves riding up and down in some pretty big swells. As I looked up at the waves I was impressed by how well the giant canoe handled the seas, even though we got wet a few times.

We didn't go far out into the blue before our guide told us to put our lines in the water. Remember, this was a primitive fishing expedition and we didn't have a clear idea of what types of fish we might catch. So we put out one big bait and one smaller bait. We weren't picky; we just wanted to catch fish—any fish!

With two lines in the water we began trolling parallel to the beautiful Bali coastline. I was in heaven; hanging out with my best friend who had become my bride, and pondering some of the bluest water imaginable while waiting for a strike. What more could a man ask for? Okay, a few fish would be nice! With the boat rhythmically rising and falling in the swells we came across a school of small tuna. Mary hooked up with a nice one and battled for a few minutes when suddenly the fight ended. Reeling in a limp line all she found attached to her hook was a head. Apparently, we were not the only predator hunting the tuna. Rather than joining us for a sashimi dinner, the poor fellow met a gruesome and toothy end.

Mary had not paid much attention to the rising and falling of the waves but with indisputable evidence of a toothy intruder lurking below, she began to cast a wary eye at the low freeboard of the giant canoe. Was it a shark? Maybe a big barracuda? We tried to catch the larger predators lurking below, but only hooked up with the smallish tuna, keeping a few for dinner. We left the school of tuna (or did they leave us?) and continued trolling along the beautiful coastline. Fishing was a bit slow but toward the end of our time we latched onto a very athletic barracuda that almost jumped over the outrigger. I've wondered if the fish we took back were the only ones ever cleaned in the bathtub of our five-star hotel room!

Our Indonesian fishing experience reminds me of how fortunate we are to fish on modern sport fishing vessels. After all, from a fisherman's perspective, a boat is vital for success. Whether it is Haleem and his ancient looking green vessel in the Maldives, our Indonesian guide on his oversized outrigger canoe or my buddy Arnie on his tricked out, 36-foot diesel-powered battlewagon, fishermen around the world rely on their vessels to take them beyond the reach of the shoreline in search of fish.

Having fished in many locations around the world, I've come to appreciate that boats, like people, are created in a variety of shapes, sizes and colors. Some are rather fragile and best suited for shallow water. If they are caught offshore in an unexpected storm, the waves will quickly consume them. Some are designed to withstand long journeys into uncharted deep water. Then there are those durable and versatile multi-purpose models, like the Indonesian outrigger canoe, which may not look like much, but whether you are trolling in minimal swell or navigating across treacherous water, these boats do it all!

Did you know that you can find a number of boating and fishing stories in the Bible? Storms, shipwrecks, catastrophic floods, fishless nights, sunrises and bountiful catches are a part of God's Word. This really shouldn't be a surprise. Water covers three-quarters of the earth's surface and more than 28,000 different species of fish swim in these rivers, lakes and seas. What may surprise you is that the central character of the Bible, Jesus Christ, spent much of his time hanging around with fishermen. Spend a little time in the Bible and you will discover that Jesus was not a stranger to water, boats or fish. He grew up in Galilee, a region famous for its highly productive commercial fishing industry. Several of his closest friends, Peter, Andrew, James and John even made their living as fishermen!

What do you think it would have been like to fish with Jesus? I doubt he was a fair-weather fisherman. According to the Bible, Jesus and his friends had some close calls with the weather over 2,000 years ago. Like the night they were crossing the lake when a ferocious storm whipped the lake into a chaotic fury of waves that were crashing over the side of their boat. Jesus used his unique "navigational skills" to get the crew out of that storm (Mark 4:35-41)!

I can't help but wonder if the boats I saw and fished on in Bali and the Maldives were similar to the boats that fishermen used during biblical times on the Sea of Galilee (minus the engines, of course). Those traditional fishing boats and the methods of anglers who make their living on them are effective yet primitive compared to a modern mechanized fishing vessel and today's techniques. When modern trawlers harvest fish, the catch is quickly processed and stored or flash frozen in massive freezers.

The ancient fishing experience on the Sea of Galilee must have been similar to my Maldivian experience. When I watched the commercial fishermen return to the docks, the floors of their boats were covered with fish. Just like today's Maldivian fishermen, first century Galileans like Peter most likely stored the fish they caught on the floor of the boat. How many fish do you think Peter jumped over as he ran around his boat, hauling in nets and securing lines? When a Galilean fisherman returned home and his sandals smelled of fish, his wife knew the catching was good!

Reading the Bible stories from the Sea of Galilee, I often wonder what Peter's boat was like. A discovery made in 1986 gives us a good idea. Archaeologists working along the shores of Galilee unearthed an ancient boat dated back to the first century. Scholars believe it was typical of the vessels used during the time of Jesus. It was 26.5 feet long, 7.5 feet wide and 4.5 feet deep. Constructed primarily of cedar planks and an oak frame, this boat used wind and oars for propulsion. The gunnels were low, making it easier to haul heavy nets laden with wiggling fish over the side. These low gunnels also increased the risk to the men on-board as the waves were that much closer. This reconstructed, wooden Galilean fishing boat is as basic as a fishing craft can get. It makes the modern, custom-built charter boats of today look like space ships.

My Indonesian and Maldivian fishing friends and the ancient Galilean fishermen certainly have some things in common. Their boats were primitive but dependable; and both had to rely on their instincts and experience to locate fish. No GPS. No sonar. No computer-enhanced topographical maps. No Internet fishing hotlines. It was (and is) truly man against fish and the environment. And on some days, all the forces of nature aligned against them. What a challenge those ancient anglers faced every time they took to the water!

Today, we anglers depend so much on our electronics that I won-der if we have lost something, perhaps dulled our natural ability to intuitively read the water and surrounding environment. In the past, observational skills and gut-level perception led fishermen to the fish. Sure, technology can help you catch more fish, but do you think tech-nology has in some ways separated us fishermen from our environment and the fish we seek? Are we less aware of our environment, and how fish react to subtle changes in their surroundings and weather, than our ancient fishing brethren were?

What would happen to the size and quantity of your catch if you left your electronics at home? Could you catch fish with only a mini-mal selection of your favorite tackle? What would happen if you went out on a lake, stream or ocean and just simply fished? Just like Peter, you against the fish: you against nature?

Let's travel back in time to the first century and visit that ancient fishery on the Sea of Galilee. This lake has attracted the attention of scholars, historians, archaeologists and theologians for ages. Why? This was the lake on which Jesus walked (yes, you read that right). This was the lake where Jesus miraculously fed more than 5,000 people with a young boy's lunch of two fish and five loaves of bread. This was the lake where Jesus spent much of his time during his earthly ministry and where he performed many miracles. And yes, this is the lake where Jesus went fishing.

> *Twenty years from now you will be more disappointed by the things that you didn't do than by the ones you did do. So throw off the bowlines. Sail away from the safe harbor. Catch the trade winds in your sails. Explore. Dream. Discover.*
>
> *—MARK TWAIN*

6

Look Beneath
the Surface

We are not afraid of the sea; we are terrified of the water.
—ANDY HILLSTRAND

There's a fine line between loyalty and stupidity.
—EDGAR HANSEN

I'm on a carnival ride in Hell now.
—RUSSELL NEWBERRY

You got to be a little bit twisted to do this job.
—PHIL HARRIS

Deadliest Catch

For the most part, I don't like reality TV shows, except for *Deadliest Catch*. That show has mesmerized me from the first time I saw it! I wanted to book a flight to Alaska and sign onto Sig Hansen's boat. I even told my wife that if I ever have a mid life crisis, she could look for me in Alaska.

Deadliest Catch brings extreme fishing into your living room as camera crews follow a handful of crab boats during the highly competitive and dangerous Alaskan crab season. Each adventure places us on the deck of a commercial fishing vessel on Alaska's notorious Bering Sea. Viewers are treated to an hour of towering waves the size of four-story buildings trying to wash men from the decks. Ice encrusts boats, equipment fails and the occasional man goes overboard, all while 500-pound crab traps crash across the decks. The viewer feels the crews' adrenaline rush from a heavy catch as well as the empty, disappointing feeling of empty pots.

As I sit in the comfort of my climate-controlled home watching these brave men struggle against the forces of nature, a part of me wants to join them. I want to stand at the helm with Sig and strategize against the weather, the fleet and the elusive Alaskan crabs. I want to put on my foul weather gear and head out on deck with Edgar Hansen and take my chances with the waves, ice and Alaska's crab regulations. Alaskan crab-fishing itself is like a boat race and a big-money lottery rolled into one. Each season sees its winners and losers as the Alaska Department of Wildlife sets the quota for the catch, issues the licenses and then sets the season—a veritable line in time. When the clock starts, the boats race off to the grounds and fish as hard as they can until the cumulative quota is met.

The Bering Sea gives no second chances. If 60-knot winds and 40-foot waves are bearing down on the fleet, hang on boys, because we're going fishing! Ice entombs boats, its massive weight making a capsize imminent, but still, the crewmembers persevere, attacking it with sledgehammers and axes. They will travel hundreds of miles across open water straight into the teeth of a raging storm and towering waves to reach the fishing grounds.

Living at sea for days and weeks on a boat that never stops moving and is constantly at the mercy of violent weather is not for the weak hearted. Once they reach the fishing grounds crews may work 24 hours without rest, setting and hauling "strings" of pots. If the captain picks the wrong area, the string, which may contain more than 100 pots, comes up nearly empty and is a bust. If the string is set on an area rich in crabs, well, it's sort of like old time miners hitting the mother lode of gold. When an Alaskan crab boat returns to port with a full load of crabs, the captain and crewmembers will make tens of thousands of dollars for a few days work.

Why is this show so fascinating? I think it's because it speaks to a deeper longing that resonates in men. It mixes the inherent uncertainty and unpredictability of fishing, the challenges of fishing in extreme weather and massive waves with the anticipation of the catch. Then it adds touches of competition and suspense and tosses in liberal doses of human quirkiness that simply captivate us. Even my oldest daughter, Rebecca, likes this show.

Commercial fishing has always been one of the most uncertain and risky occupations on the face of the earth. The show masterfully illustrates the tension between ever-present, life-threatening dangers and the potential monetary reward that awaits those who make the big haul. Does this remind you of how life's storms and challenges stretch our character?

While *Deadliest Catch* may be an extreme example, fishing truly is an unpredictable and risky occupation. Whether on the open ocean or inland lakes and rivers fishermen face a multitude of hostile variables that can wreak havoc on their gear, mind, body and pocketbook. From unpredictable and dangerous weather to fluctuating fish stocks to equipment failure to market pressures, the fishing industry has no guarantees.

If you make your living ashore you probably can go to work almost every day without much concern for the wind and weather. Not so a fisherman. Every day a fisherman must wonder, "Will the weather allow me to get to the fish? Where will the fish be—has wind and current moved them? Will the rigging and gear function properly? Will I make any money today?"

As rugged, unpredictable and dangerous as fishing on *Deadliest Catch* is, what do you suppose commercial fishing was like during the first century? I imagine that an ancient fisherman never stopped thinking about the weather, or its impact on the fish. Today, we depend on technology for our forecasts but a first century fisherman had to rely solely on his instincts. Day and night, his eyes would watch the sky for signs of change. He would intuitively observe subtle changes in cloud texture, sky color and wind shifts. Ancient fishermen would be so in tune with the weather and its impact on the fish that they would instinctively know how the day's hunt would unfold simply by the aroma in the air and the touch of the wind on their skin in the morning. Primitive anglers were led to fish by instincts honed over time. Fishing was truly man against nature!

Tackle companies may introduce new and improved gear every year, but the truth is, fishing is an ancient occupation that has been around for a very, very long time. It was an important industry in the Middle East during the first century. The ancient Jewish historian, Josephus, reports that the Sea of Galilee was home to a thriving commercial fishing industry and included 230 boats during the time of Christ. The dominant species of fish caught were freshwater sardines, barbels and musht, which were harvested by drag, dip and gill nets as well as a little hook and line fishing.

Located in the Jordan Rift Valley at 600 feet below sea level, the Sea of Galilee is 13 miles long, 8 miles wide and reaches a maximum depth of 150 feet. Also known as the Sea of Tiberias, this inland freshwater sea is well respected for three things: beautiful surroundings, fertile waters, and its unpredictable and highly volatile personality.

Geographically, the Sea of Galilee is uniquely positioned to facilitate the development of the perfect storm. The unpredictable seas and rough waters are created by a local wind phenomenon known as Ventures. Oceanic winds roar in off the Mediterranean Sea just 22 miles away and pick up velocity as they funnel though the Arbell Pass at the northwest corner of the lake. Since the lake is aligned north and south, these bursts of wind quickly whip the water into a fury of seething waves.

Sudden and unpredictable bursts of wind and waves make the waters a nautical nightmare and must have wreaked havoc on ancient Galilean fishermen. Have you ever been on open water when a storm came racing in? It's scary enough to race it to shore when you have gas engines roaring. Imagine being under sail or oar power, tending nets 2,000 years ago when a rapidly advancing squall full of lightning and thunder appeared. You had no weather channel or color radar to warn of the approaching danger. Any trip out in your wooden boat could have been your last. Those guys lived in the immediacy of the present and this unique environment taught fishermen to closely observe every facet of their surroundings.

A Band of Fishermen

I believe it is no coincidence that a rag-tag group of these ancient fisher-men became central characters in the gospel narrative of Jesus Christ. When Jesus began his earthly ministry in primitive Palestine he chose a group of 12 men to be his students, or "disciples." Following first century cultural customs these men followed Jesus and spent a great deal of time with him. At least four of the 12 disciples, Peter, John, James and Andrew, made their living as fishermen. Some scholars have speculated that three additional disciples, Thomas, Nathaniel and Philip were also fishermen.

These men Jesus chose were not religiously trained theologians or philosophers. They were fishermen. Fishing was not something these men did on the weekend to unwind or to avoid a honey-do-list or as a source of escape from the cares of the world. Fishing was a rugged and deadly undertaking that they did day after day to pay the rent, clothe their children and put food on the table. And they did it on the treacherous Sea of Galilee. Out of all humanity, these were the men Christ chose to reveal both his true identity and his revolutionary rescue plan.

So, why did Jesus choose fishermen? Is it their clear, penetrating vision that allows them to peer deeply into the unseen mysteries of life? On the water, fishermen visualize the unseen world beneath the surface and each day can become a journey of discovery. After all, there's a lot more to this world than meets the eye and when we step away from all the *noise* and gadgets that can consume our time we often see opportunities, relationships and beauty that otherwise goes unnoticed.

Fishing also teaches life skills such as patience and self-control. One who makes his living on the water is not afraid of hard work, long hours, unexpected challenges or extreme working conditions.

Having made my living by fishing for more than 25 years, it thrills me that this core group of men contained several fishermen. What was Jesus thinking? He handpicked these 12 men himself. I wonder what he saw? Was there a little bit of you and me in each of these men? Men with a past? Men with scars and wounds? Men with dreams and passions? Men with potential?

Whatever it was, Jesus strolled down to the shoreline one day and met two of the disciples, Peter and John, right where they lived. He didn't call them to the local synagogue. He didn't ask them to fill out an application or jump through hoops of religiosity. Personality and spirituality tests were not required. They were not political or military leaders. They were not scholars or theologians. They were not educated, rich or influential men. These were two ordinary, hardworking men from the backwater town of Galilee who happened to be partners in a fishing business. They spent their time repairing nets and boats, hauling fish from choppy waters and cleaning them. And they were far from perfect. Peter often resembled a heat-seeking missile with his choice of words. John and his brother James had a rather ominous nickname, the "Sons of Thunder". What stories do you suppose stand behind a name that sounds like a motorcycle gang? Despite their issues, Jesus simply got on their boats one day, pushed off into deep waters and went fishing.

When the trip was over—a hugely successful trip—Peter and John left their nets and embarked on a journey of faith. This journey began at the water's edge and led these men away from the life they knew and down a path filled with uncertainty, storms, temptation, suffering, boredom, disappointment, risk, danger and most certainly excitement. Sound a bit like a fishing trip?

What Did They See?

Just like us, they had choices to make; especially when following Jesus got hard. When the going got tough, Peter and John were always free to walk away from Jesus—but they didn't! Despite what the crowds said, despite what the culture thought, these men remained by Jesus' side—even in the face of death. And through the struggles of life, Jesus forged a unique relationship with these men that altered their course forever. At first Jesus was a stranger to Peter and John. But over time, they became friends as they experienced life together. You see, Jesus didn't just hang out with the disciples, sipping cappuccinos at a Mediterranean sidewalk café discussing the latest trends. He patiently invested time in them—building relationships, mentoring, teaching and doing life together.

These men weren't watching the highlights on the 10 o'clock news—they were on the front lines. For nearly three years, through the dark of night and the heat of the day, they followed Jesus. They routinely hiked across the rugged Judean countryside and traversed stormy seas in small boats with him. They had a front row seat as Jesus confronted the political authorities and challenged the social structures of the day. They witnessed the supernatural power of his miracles as he turned water into wine, restored sight to the blind, gave voice to the mute, fed the hungry, healed the lame and sick and even raised the dead. Scripture tells us these men even went on to perform miracles themselves.

I have no doubt that the disciples not only knew Jesus well, but that they scrutinized him closely too. We all know actions speak louder than words. And, it's a given that the more time you spend with someone the better you know them. While Jesus made some big claims about *who* he was, he backed up his claims with actions that proved he was no ordinary man.

Some of my friends are well known and dare I say *famous* fishermen . . . but I've never seen any of them walk on the water or calm a raging sea. And some of my friends pack a mean spread for a day on the water but they've never fed a few thousand people with a sack lunch. And yes, some of my friends enjoy a good brew or a glass of fine wine, but even in a tough economy they can't change the water into anything else but ice or steam and they need a freezer or stove to do that.

Jesus was no ordinary man, and it's pretty clear that being around Jesus transformed these ordinary fishermen. These unlikely characters who once made their living pulling fish from a treacherous inland sea went on to turn the world upside down with the life-changing message of the gospel. Two thousand years later we can still see Jesus through their experiences that are recorded in the Bible. Two of these fishermen,

John and Peter, actually wrote several of the books found in the Bible's New Testament. John wrote the Gospel of John, three short letters (1, 2 and 3 John) and the Revelation. Peter left us two letters, 1 and 2 Peter. Many scholars also believe the Gospel of Mark is based on Peter's eyewitness accounts of his time with Jesus. Insightful references to Peter and John can also be found in the book of Acts.

While we can learn much from their experiences with Jesus, I hope you realize how much we have in common with Peter and John. We love the thrill of seeking an unseen adversary lurking beneath the waves, and just being outdoors quickens our pulse and makes us feel more alive.

Something that makes fishermen unique is that we're closer to nature than much of humankind. We intuitively observe our environment, developing an uncanny sense, a sort of internal radar that helps us to sense life at a deeper level. When a fisherman heads out on the water for a day of fishing, he doesn't *see* the fish but he has faith that he will catch them. After all, a fisherman not only *sees* and *experiences* the unseen day after day—he *believes* in the unseen. Fishing teaches us to look beyond ourselves and to have faith.

Fishing taught Peter and John to look beneath the surface and to see deeper truths. We may not know why Jesus would choose such ordinary men as his disciples (other than that he liked them!) but it's pretty clear Peter and John felt they had good reason to choose Jesus. Are you at all curious about what they saw in Jesus? Are you at all interested in *who* Jesus is and the promises he made for you? Let's load the boats and head offshore alongside these ancient fishermen and see what we can learn from their experiences. I bet Peter wouldn't mind if we helped him pull a few nets.

*Seventeen vessels and 209 lives have been lost in the
Gloucester fisheries during the year. Forty of the men are
known to have left widows, and the number of fatherless
children of which there is a record is 68. Seventy-one men
capsized or gone astray in dories have reached the shore
or been rescued from a watery grave, many of them
after exposure and sufferings that defy description.*

—JOSEPH E. GARLAND

Cape Ann Weekly Advertiser, January 4, 1884

The Lone Voyager

7

The Great Catch

A thousand fishing trips go by, indistinguishable
from one another, and then suddenly one
comes along that is fatefully perfect.
—A. J. McClane

Fishing captains are hunters at heart. While most people go to work at a set destination, the place where I do the most business changes location from day to day and hour to hour. My office is where the fish are. And, as you most certainly have discovered, fish have a crazy habit of changing locations just when you think you've figured them out. Some days it seems like the fish have roller skates on because they move around so much. To survive in the fishing business, I must locate schools of fish, day in and day out.

On one particular day, I was watching the sonar closely for signs of life as my 30-foot Pursuit, the *Blue Horizon,* (the *Blue Horizon* was my fourth charter boat) ran offshore in search of the mighty king salmon. It was a typical summer morning—a magenta tint reflecting off the building cumulus clouds and light, southerly winds caressing the cool waters of Lake Michigan into a light chop. With six enthusiastic clients barraging me with questions, my mind was focused on *the hunt*—locating the big schools of mature king salmon that were staging for their fall spawning run. Setting up on top of a school of feeding fish makes me look like a hero—and leads to return business. When I crossed 80 feet of water, I turned the boat to the north and ran a zigzag course parallel to a sharp drop off. Schools of baitfish would frequently hold along this ledge in 70 to 120 feet of water. If the sonar lit up, it was time to go to work! If I didn't mark the bait stacks, then I would run further offshore, continuing the search for bait and game-fish, which would show as marks on my sonar's LCD screen.

When hunting summer kings, baitfish and ice cold water are the ingredients for success, and modern sonar and temperature probes help us find both. Well, on this day we found acres of bait just beyond the 100-foot line. As we idled down, I launched a pair of wire divers rigged with flashers and flies. With the divers slipping out against the drag, I began setting the downriggers. Before the second rigger had reached the target depth 65 feet down, both diver rigs began *screaming* as two large kings crushed the baits. The back deck turned to chaos as the quick action caught my donut-munching clients by surprise! As they debated who should fight the fish, one of the rigger rods began bucking in the holder as a third king slammed the fly. Welcome to my world!

Isn't technology amazing! Before the first line hits the water, I can run my charter boat across open water at high speeds and know if any fish are present. Modern technology gives us a competitive edge and has changed the way we go fishing. Today, sport and commercial fishermen rely on a variety of high-tech electronics such as computer-enhanced topographical charts, GPS, chart plotters, radar, sonar, side-scanning sonar, sub-surface temperature and speed probes, underwater cameras, and cell phones to help locate fish. But even with all this technology, some days we just can't find the fish. And even when we do find them, we can't always make them strike.

If you journey back in time, you will find that men have been harvesting fish from the oceans, lakes and rivers for ages without high-tech tools of any sort. References to fishing in art date back 4,000 years in Egyptian, Chinese, Greek, Assyrian, Roman and Jewish cultures. A Chinese account from the 4th century B.C. refers to fishing with a silk line, a bamboo rod and cooked rice as bait.

I imagine that life as a vocational fisherman during the first century was rugged, physically demanding and filled with uncertainty. Just like today's professional anglers, experience taught our fishing ancestors that the day's wages were as unpredictable as the weather. By today's standards, finding and catching fish must have been incredibly challenging for our ancient ancestors. It must have made tough men even tougher.

This was certainly true for those who made a living seeking fish from the highly volatile Sea of Galilee. A Galilean fisherman faced long hours, backbreaking work and an unpredictable and dangerous work environment. Years of hauling heavy nets from the depths would have firmly sculpted his arms. Tawny legs with the strength of cedar beams would be finely tuned from standing and bracing one's body on the deck of a pitching and heaving boat. Large, calloused hands would have the strength of an eagle's claw. Matted hair, tangled from the unceasing wind, would frame a weather-beaten face deeply marked by long hours under a hot sun.

In the pages of the Bible we meet a man who most likely fit this description. With the waves melting into the shoreline we find Simon Peter washing his nets after a long, fishless night. This surprising story of Jesus calling Peter along the shoreline is found in three of the Gospels—Matthew, Mark and Luke. While the theme and message are consistent, each writer presents a slightly different angle on this story. Matthew and Mark focus on the call and the response: *"Come, follow me . . . and immediately they left everything and followed."*

More to the Story Than Meets the Eye

But there's much more to the story. Luke takes a deeper look into Peter's character, examining the underlying tension when he first met Jesus.

Luke was a physician who thoroughly investigated the life of Jesus and wrote an "orderly account" of "the things that have been accomplished among us" (Luke 1). When Luke picks up the story, we find Jesus on the shore of the Sea of Galilee. A large crowd of eager fans was following him, hoping to witness one of his miracles or hear his latest controversial teachings. As Jesus walks down the shoreline he draws our attention to two boats on the beach (Luke 5:2). Notice that at the time the boats were empty of men and fish.

Fishing was finished for the night (the most productive fishing on Galilee was during nighttime hours). Peter and his brother Andrew were washing their nets, stowing their gear and, undoubtedly, discussing their strategy for the evening trip. The previous night's hunt had been tough—okay, let's be real, it stunk! *They caught nothing.* When you fish for a living, you never stop thinking about the fish or the water: Your mind is constantly contemplating your next move. We anglers of today can imagine what Peter and Andrew were talking about after this lousy night of fishing. "How are we going to do better tonight? Should we try a different part of the lake? Did a weather change put the fish down? Did you hear what the Ben Abraham brothers caught? Didn't the new guy from Bethsaida use a drag net last year at this time when the fishing got really tough?"

As the two brothers contemplate their next move and think up excuses to explain their fishless night, along comes the carpenter, Jesus of Nazareth. As Jesus approaches Peter, he looks first at the empty boats. Then he asks the fisherman, Peter, to get back into one of the vessels. Now Peter had just spent a fishless night in that boat, and I imagine, if he were anything like me, he didn't want anything to do with that boat right then. After a tough day on the water, I know I want to get as far away from my boat as possible!

Peter, however, does what Jesus asks. He gets back in the boat. This outing turned out very different than his previous fishing trip. Jesus simply asks Peter to take him, and his boat, a short distance from the shoreline where he turns Peter's boat into a floating pulpit so he can speak to the crowd. I can picture Peter positioning his boat in a small cove and the people lining the edges of the beach. What a peaceful and natural setting in which to learn! The placid waters would convey Jesus' words clearly to the people gathered along the shoreline. *This is certainly easier than fishing,* thinks Peter as he reclines in the stern of the boat.

Luke doesn't tell us how long the impromptu lesson lasts but when the class comes to an end, Jesus turns his attention on one man—Simon Peter. Jesus looks at Peter, who may have been relaxing in the stern listening to Jesus (and maybe still contemplating what went wrong the night before), and simply commands him, "Simon, put out into the deep and let down your nets for a catch."

After the fishless night how do you think Peter feels at the prospect of going back out on the water? And hadn't he just washed those nets, folded them and stowed them away? But, look closely at the words Jesus uses. He not only tells Peter *when* to go fishing, again, but he tells him *where* to go—into the deep. He also makes a promise of success for he tells Peter, "You will catch many fish" (NLT).

Now, I've been guiding clients for more years than I care to remember and nothing irks me more than a doctor, lawyer, or computer geek telling me how or where to fish. The nerve! It really gets under my skin. I don't tell them how to defend a client or remove a gall bladder. What gives them the right to tell me how to do MY job? How do you think Peter, the experienced fisherman on the boat, feels when this carpenter tells him to drop his nets in deep water?

For all the times in the Bible Peter would fire off a verbal heat-seeking missile in later accounts, he remains incredibly composed and respectful on this day. He graciously reminds Jesus that he had "toiled all night and took nothing! But, at your word I will let down the nets." As Peter goes along with Jesus' command, what do you suppose he was thinking? *Another empty net? Fool, doesn't he know there are no fish here? I don't tell him how to hammer pegs and make tables. This crazy carpenter-turned-rabbi wants to change professions, again?*

Pause for a moment—what did Peter know of Jesus at this point in his journey? In Luke 5:5 he calls Jesus "Master," but as far as we know, he had not been invited to follow him yet. He may have heard of some of Jesus' teachings or about the miracles that he had performed in the region, but he most likely had little, if any experience with Jesus. He knew little about Jesus, but he obeyed him. Despite an entire night's futile effort and any skepticism on Peter's part, he is willing to try again. Peter trusts Jesus and has faith in his words. Peter goes out into the deep water after a hard night's work and puts down his net once again.

Fishing by Faith

This fishing excursion to deep water was Peter's first step of faith. But what if he missed this opportunity? What if a stubborn and weary spirit caused him to stay on the beach?

But he didn't. Simon steps into his boat, and what a step it turns out to be! Jesus looks across the water and tells Peter to move the boat, drop the net, then brace yourself man—you are going to catch some fish. And catch fish they do! The text tells us they fill the boat, literally! They catch so many fish the gear can't handle the strain—"They enclosed a large number of fish, and their nets were breaking." I would have loved to see the look on Peter's face as he dropped the net over the side and then suddenly felt the weight of the heaving net full of struggling fish pulling against his arms and hands. The net was so full of fish that the boat probably listed to the side. How do you think Peter responded? I bet he belted out a scream of excitement and joy that was heard all the way to Jerusalem!

From Peter's response, we know this was no ordinary catch, and certainly unexpected. The text tells us that Peter and all who saw this event (including James and John) were *astonished* or *awestruck*. When Jesus went fishing, records were crushed. The catch was so large that Peter had to call for a second boat to help bring the fish to shore. "They signaled to their partners in the other boat to come and help them. And they came and filled both the boats, so that they began to sink" (Luke 5:7).

When was the last time you needed a second boat to haul your catch back to port? When was the last time you sank your boat with fish? I've made some huge catches of fish, like the time Ron Berg and I had a stringer of massive fall-run kings lashed to the side of a canoe. Or the morning we were catching dorado as fast as we could drop our lines in the water. Yet, I never have come close to swamping from the weight of the catch. Of course I follow state creel limits and only keep what the law allows, but even if I didn't, I can't imagine having to call for a second boat to help carry the catch back to port. No doubt, this catch of fish exceeded anything that Peter ever had anticipated, let alone previously experienced.

After being skunked only a few hours earlier, what do you suppose Peter was thinking *now*?

Me? I might have been overly impressed with my own fishing skills. Would I tell my buddies, or keep the spot a secret? Or, would I be thinking about the fat paycheck the catch would bring or maybe I should build a larger boat to hold more fish? Or I might be planning my next trip back to this new secret spot.

But Peter was no fool, he hadn't forgotten about the previous night's failure and the empty net. He knew the best fishing was during the night. But now, in the middle of the day, Jesus (the carpenter) shows up, tells Peter to reposition the boat, drop the net and wham! The net is instantly full—fish flop everywhere, gunnels to gunnels, nothing but fish! So many that a second boat is needed to haul the catch to shore!

Peter may have had a stormy personality, but he wasn't an idiot. He knew he was not responsible for the great catch. As a result, Peter did not focus on the fish. Rather, his focus was on the man responsible for the great catch—Jesus. In response to this unprecedented haul, Peter, the seasoned fishing pro, didn't pound his chest proclaiming *his* greatness. He didn't call the local paper to brag. He "fell down at Jesus' knees, saying, Oh, Lord, please leave me—I'm too much of a sinner to be around you" (Luke 5:8 NLT).

Who Is This Man?

What an amazing response! Peter made his living catching fish and it must have taken a lot to get him excited. But on this day his ego was buried on the bottom of the lake. Peter was overcome and filled with awe. Peter knew the lake and the habits and patterns of the fish intimately. He realized something very unusual and supernatural had just occurred in his midst. He knew Jesus had miraculously drawn those fish to one place and filled his net. What was going on? Who was this man Jesus?

Peter's journey was only just beginning. But he knew that, on this day, he was in the presence of a holy man like no other. What else could Peter do but fall prostrate on his face in amazement, wonder, awe and fear? How would you respond if you met Jesus?

This great catch of fish not only tore the net, it ripped to the core of Peter's very being. On this day the eyes of Peter's heart were opened and in humility he recognized the tension between Jesus and him—his own sin. Fishermen know that extreme tension can break even the strongest fishing line and Peter was broken when he said, "I'm too much of a sinner to be around you."

Peter was a first century Jew. Culturally, he would have been raised to read, memorize and recite Scripture. Most likely, he had been taught the story of Adam and Eve and the first sin. But it didn't mean anything—until the day Jesus filled his boat with fish. Suddenly, after a fishless night and the unexpected tug of a net, the ancient Scriptures didn't appear quite so distant. For Peter, this day went beyond any religious doctrine he had memorized. On this day, his net ripped and his heart was torn open. For the first time, Peter realized that a gap existed between him and God. His sin separated him from God.

I put it to you that, just like Peter's relationship, our relationship with God is broken by our sin. Just like a broken fishing line, we are not connected to God as we should be. According to the first book of the Bible, Genesis, there was a time when a man named Adam walked in perfect peace with God. Adam's direct relationship with God was like an unbroken fishing line. This perfect vertical relationship, however, was broken when Adam sinned. Sadly, that fractured relationship has been passed down to all of his descendants, including you and me. We'll take a closer look at this in chapter 9.

On this day Peter was confronted by Truth. He was overcome and distressed by an acute awareness of his sin. In the presence of Jesus

Christ, he knew that something dark and hideous—his sin—separated him from God. How would you respond if God met you on your boat, the dock, or shoreline; and he exposed your sin for what it is? Peter responded in honest fear when he asked Jesus to *leave* or *depart* from him. It's not that Peter didn't admire Jesus; he was convicted of Jesus' glory and his divine power. But, this conviction brought Peter to his knees in humility because he was aware of his unworthiness to be in God's perfect presence.

Like many of us, Peter's first reaction in light of this profound moment was to ask Jesus to leave. He did not yet understand why Jesus had climbed aboard his boat. Peter knew that Jesus was unlike any other man. But he didn't know that Jesus was standing in his boat on purpose; that he came into the world to seek the lost, like Peter . . . you . . . and me. Jesus came to restore broken relationships between God and humanity.

The people who hung out with Jesus understood this better than anyone. One of Peter's best friends, Paul, tells us that on our own we are all unworthy to stand in the presence of God (Romans 3:10-12). Sounds like an impossible position to be in, but Peter tells us that there is a solution. In a letter he wrote, he tells us that Jesus made a way for us to approach God in peace (1 Peter 3:18). Peter discovered that Jesus repairs broken relationships with God as fully as if he'd cleared the old, rotten line from our tangled reel and filled our spool with a super-line that can never break—no matter how great the challenge. Peter learned that Jesus paid our debt of failures and rebellion, and ransomed us from the deadly and eternal jaws of sin. He alone was worthy of stepping into the gap that sin had torn between God and humanity. Later we will examine why Jesus had to pay our debt, but right now, let's see what else we can learn from Peter's first encounter with Jesus.

After the nets had been pulled, Peter's heart was aching. He was filled with a deep awareness of his sin and he knew Jesus was unlike any other man. But he still didn't quite get it. The wheels were turning, but Peter did not fully understand why Jesus had come into the world. On the day that Peter, the professional fisherman, was handed a boatload of fish by someone who was clearly more than just a carpenter turned rabbi—his heart was awakened! Jesus came into the world to save sinners like him.

Is God Looking for You?

Have you thought about *where* all this "religious stuff" happened to him? Jesus made a profound impact on Peter in familiar territory—the deck of a fishing boat. We so often think we have to go to a building, a church, to meet with God. We limit God to one physical location! But nothing could be further from the truth. Peter learned that God is not confined to a building or held captive by a temporal schedule. God created you and he knows what makes you tick. He knows what course you've charted and he seeks you in the midst of your journey.

God has a personal plan for you, just like he did for Peter. Peter learned that to join God's team he had to step aside and allow Jesus to take control of the helm. If we allow God to set the coordinates on the GPS of our lives' we begin to live in true freedom, just like Peter.

Let me explain. Jesus didn't want to be Peter's first mate. He wanted to be Peter's captain. Jesus allowed Peter to struggle and fail at what he knew best, fishing. Jesus then showed Peter what the results would look like if he aligned his will with God's. When Peter let Jesus direct his boat out into deep water, his nets could not contain the blessing that Jesus poured out on him.

Do you think the same is true for you and me? Do we limit God? Do we keep him at a safe distance? If we ask Jesus to be our first mate we may *feel* better for a while, but we won't be any different. We won't experience the life-changing power that only comes through an authentic relationship with Jesus Christ. As Peter learned, if we want to fully and completely engage with Jesus, we must surrender control of our desires, struggles and destiny to him. This begins in the heart and leads to a turning that penetrates every aspect of our life and actions. Complete trust leads to transformation.

God made this profound impression on Peter the fisherman while he was engaged in his vocation. In a way that Peter could understand, he dramatically showed him how futile his *own* efforts were. He let Peter go fishing, and he let him fail. Then Jesus gave a command and Peter's obedience led him to the catch of his life! Through the events of that day, Jesus told Peter, "If you will only trust me, your nets would be overflowing!" Jesus met Peter on the water, re-calibrated his heart, and gave him new direction in his life. Jesus also gave Peter the courage and strength to follow when he said, "Don't be afraid! From now on you'll be fishing for people! And as soon as they landed, they left everything and followed Jesus" (Luke 5:10 NLT).

This was only just the beginning, but what a way to begin! Peter was a man chosen by God to stand on the front line. He was an eyewitness to the life, ministry, death and resurrection of Jesus. Peter says, "We were witnesses of all that he (Jesus) did both in the country of the Jews and in Jerusalem" (Acts 10:3).

Peter calls out to us through the cobwebs of time and asks us to join him. He challenges us to open the eyes of our heart and to journey with him. Peter witnessed many sunrises and sunsets with the Lord. He journeyed across the rugged terrain of primitive Palestine, broke bread with Jesus, shared stories, laughter and tears, and sailed through storms on the Sea of Galilee. He watched Jesus heal the sick, the lame and the lost. He watched as Jesus challenged the political authorities and the power systems of the day. He witnessed Jesus' death. And then he saw the risen Jesus—ALIVE. Peter saw and believed the evidence; Jesus had defeated death. He finally understood that Jesus died for him. And it completely changed his life.

Peter spent the rest of his earthly life taking this message to the world. He went *out into the deep water* in obedience.

What about us? Are we willing to step away from the safe, shallow waters and follow Jesus into deep water? Or, do we hang around the shallow shoreline where it's "safe?" When Peter obeyed, God's blessing exceeded his wildest dreams.

Peter's steps of faith were not always easy. In fact, he faced many difficult challenges and he was no Superman. Truth is, he was a lot like us—he often failed. But Jesus always reinstated him. While none of us like to fail, life will present us all with a variety of challenges that complicate our lives and, at times, get the best of us. Peter knew this all too well; he was a fisherman!

Have you ever thought about past challenges you've faced on the water? Can these situations teach us or prepare us to face the challenges of life? Let me share a few of the challenges that I've encountered on my journey.

> *The fish only knows that it lives in the water, after it is*
> *already on the riverbank. Without our awareness of another*
> *world out there, it would never occur to us to change.*
> —MARK TWAIN

8

The Challenge!

*We resist the very idea of limits, regarding
limits of all sorts as temporary and
regrettable impositions on our lives.*

—Parker Palmer

Let Your Life Speak

Fishing is a challenging sport. From the moment you hit the water until the last cast, each and every fishing trip is filled with challenges. Some of these challenges will be rather mundane, like choosing between a crankbait and a jig for pre-spawn walleyes. Other challenges will be more profound—like the time my friend Joe was hooked up to an angry marlin when massive tackle failure darkened the horizon. As I learned on that day, some of the more profound challenges require us to make decisions that have far reaching consequences. Isn't that how life often works?

It was a typical day on the Pacific Ocean. Hot sun, thick, salty air and the hypnotic rhythm of the sea made a perfect setting for four sun-deprived amigos. We were trolling the fertile waters off Cabo San Lucas, Mexico, hoping to catch a striped or blue marlin. As the 31-foot Bertram sliced through the morning swells the 20-pound class Penn International suddenly started screaming—an acrobatic striped marlin had crushed the bait. Joe was up to bat and he quickly jumped on the rod and began battling the rampaging fish. After a series of spectacular leaps, the 140-pound billfish started running hard for the horizon when Joe suddenly started yelling at the crew. Something had gone terribly wrong—seems the handle had fallen off the reel! Joe was in a precarious position, tied fast to the biggest fish he'd ever seen, and this creature was rapidly peeling line off his reel. How could he ever hope to put the line back on the spool?

This was a crucial moment—for Joe and the marlin. Who would win this contest? Joe and the broken reel, or the marlin?

Well, for the mate and captain it was fourth down and 20 yards to go with time running out. They were ready to punt. With no spare handles or any extra reels on the charter boat, they saw no options. The odds were against us as the marlin continued to strip line from the disabled reel, but I was not ready to admit defeat! In gringo Spanish I excitedly exclaimed to the mate that I had a much smaller Diawa 47H levelwind reel spooled with 17-pound test line in my duffel bag. If we worked faster than any two deckhands had ever worked we could strip line off my extra reel, pull the broken reel off the rod, put the lighter, much smaller reel (with a handle) on the rod, cut the live-line with the hot fish on it, and splice the line (with the hot fish) into the backup reel and Joe could continue the battle.

The plan was quickly adopted and the captain began backing down hard on the rampaging fish. The mate and I swapped the reels—and the excitement accelerated into high gear! The mate, with a gloved hand, held the line connected to the furious fish as I cut it and spliced the two lines together. And before anyone knew what was going on, Joe was back in the game! Because of focus, fast action and a plan, our team navigated through great adversity, which helped Joe catch and release his first striped marlin.

Every fishing trip doesn't require such heroic efforts, nor end with such fantastic rewards, yet most outings require you to navigate through a variety of challenges. From the first cast to the last, fishing teaches you to make decisions and, at times, overcome adversity. Some choices are easily managed and become second nature with experience. Others, such as catching your final fish in the waning moments of a tournament or troubleshooting an outboard motor that won't start with a storm bearing down on you require a bit more effort to navigate. They can easily stretch us to our limits.

Just like Joe's crucial moment with the marlin on the Pacific, life also presents us with a variety of challenges. Many of our daily choices are routine and inconsequential. Other decisions are more complex and have a far-reaching impact on our family, friends and careers. Perhaps it is a boss who devalues you or politely tells you, "You are no longer needed." Or a financial commitment is draining the life out of you. Maybe a nagging health issue is slowing you down, or an addiction you thought you could control is slowly consuming you. It could be a wayward child or a spousal relationship that is failing. At the end of the day, you want to know all the answers and have everything resolved. *You want to control your life.* But life doesn't work like this, does it? Some things will always remain beyond your control. *What do you do with the unknowns of life?* How do you navigate from one Monday to the next when the waves of life are too big to steer around?

When confronted with equipment failure on the water we work hard to overcome adversity. If we've had a slow outing, we often seek a little advice from our fishing gurus and maybe buy a few new lures. We lick our wounds and tweak our strategy for when the sun rises, we will put our lines back in the water.

When facing challenges at home or work do we take the time to assess the consequences of our actions with as much fervor and passion? Or, do we float down the river time and eventually discover the obvious after capsizing in the rapids? If you were fishing for crappie with four-pound test and a school of toothy northern pike crossed your path, you wouldn't let the hungry pike repeatedly cut your line without adding a leader or switching to a heavier rig, would you? But sometimes we go through life beating our heads against the wall, oblivious (and not so oblivious) to changes we should make!

A World Without Limits

Do you stare defiantly into the winds of adversity, gritting your teeth and *hoping* for the best? Many men live their lives thinking they are somehow immortal and that they live in a world without limits. In *Let Your Life Speak*, Parker Palmer addresses this myth that is deeply ingrained in the American psyche. Palmer states, "we resist the very idea of limits, regarding limits of all sorts as temporary and regrettable impositions on our lives. Our national myth is about the endless defiance of limits: opening the western frontier, breaking the speed of sound, dropping people on the moon, discovering "cyberspace" at the very moment when we have filled old-fashioned space with so much junk that we can barely move. We refuse to take no for an answer."

Late night TV reinforces this idea of a world without limits. From the cradle to the grave the booming voice of pop culture tells you to "take charge, young man!" You're assaulted with messages to "seek your own voice! Control your destiny!" You're told that if you get the right degree, nothing will stand in your way. A perfect, Adonis-like body will assure you of wonderful health. And, of course, if you find the perfect spouse (who resembles the models on the beer commercials), your marriage will be perfect!

But we all eventually find out that we can't photo-shop our careers, relationships and bodies, so why not save ourselves through sound financial planning? If you make the right investments in your 401K, then you can build up a war chest that will protect you from the storms of life and guarantee yourself a peaceful and prosperous retirement.

That plan always sounds good, but I bet you know someone for whom mere accumulation of wealth hasn't worked out.

It's true, isn't it? Even if you make all the right moves at work, maintain your health, build a great investment portfolio and strive to build peaceful relationships, life will present you with challenges that are beyond your control. Go back to the launching pad when you were conceived in your mother's womb. In the womb, our physical development is dependent on our mother's personal habits and your DNA. When we are born, we submit to the process of growth, development and aging. We don't tell our body how or when to develop. As I sized up the defensive tackle staring at me across the scrimmage line in seventh grade, thinking he *belonged in ninth grade,* I wish I had been bigger and stronger. I spent most of that game getting knocked on my butt, and there was nothing I could do about it.

As children we submit to the guidance and governance of our parents. As we enter society through the school playground we submit to the rules and authority of teachers and older children. When we leave home and become citizens of a community we submit to the codes of conduct and laws of schools, companies, society and the government. Every minute of the day we submit to the law of gravity. And, on April 15, we all submit to the IRS. It is so ironic! Submission, the act of yielding control, is part of life.

Not convinced? Do you *really* think you live in a world without limits? Strip down to your skivvies, grab your high school graduation photo, then go look at yourself in the mirror—you submitted to the process of aging and you didn't even realize it! There are forces much greater than aging working on you today. Everyday, you submit to the forces, relationships and objects of this world.

Fishing is filled with challenges that don't always work out the way we desire. Even though you choose the ideal location, schedule your trip during the peak season, buy the best equipment and hire the top guide, the results are not always what you anticipated. You may do everything right while on the water but at the end of the day, you don't always find what you are looking for, do you? Like the 10-pound bass hiding behind the moss-covered stump? Or how about the 50-inch musky that sneers at you every time you visit the lake where he lives? Or the massive snook that repeatedly takes you into the mangroves. And don't forget the trophy rainbow you saw eat a butterfly and that now resides in your dreams! You know the exact spot in the run where he lives, but you can't get that beast to even look at your flies. These fish haunt your imagination. You know they exist; yet you can't quite figure out how to connect.

Likewise, life has its share of problems that try as we might, just don't work out the way we wish. When I reflect on my journey I can see how unfulfilled goals broke my heart, addictions and unhealthy habits threatened to consume me, relationships led me astray, and events that didn't seem to make any sense frequently blew me off course. Some of these problems and shortcomings were the result of external events, like the major surgery that stole a year of high school athletics from me. But many of my life's struggles were a direct reflection of me—a man with a flawed hard drive. Try as I might, I have a natural tendency to push boundaries and defy authority. To be honest, I don't always love God or my neighbor as I ought too.

Bad Genetics and Lousy Relatives

Today, it's fashionable to blame our DNA or our childhood experiences for our shortcomings as adults. Psychologists and the media tell us that there is nothing wrong with any of us. No one is ever at fault. We're all perfect, just like the models and actors on the TV screen, right? The world's problems are simply the result of bad genetics or a family's environment.

Guess what? That's exactly what the Bible says—bad genetics and lousy relatives! The Bible, however, calls it sin. No one can escape its deadly grasp. I am a flawed creature, and try as I might, will make rotten choices and sometimes do the wrong thing on purpose. Sometimes I'm just a selfish pig and it's all about me. Not even an innocent little child is free of this propensity. Hang around a playground for a moment and you will see that no one has to teach a child to break the rules; it's natural. In fact, we come off the production line *bent and broken.*

Sin is the human contradiction and the human condition. It is the cold, dark fog that creeps in between two people and destroys marriages. Sin is the anger that erodes a man's character. Sin is the lust that drains the life and vitality out of a man's soul. Sin is the pride that urges a man to sweep dark secrets under the rug. Sin is the hatred that leads a man to abuse his brother. Sin is the poverty that chokes entire villages. Sin is the greed of multi-national corporations that rape the environment of precious resources and transfer potential wealth from poor, struggling nations to the wealthy. Sin wears many faces, and frequently evades detection.

When my oldest daughter Rebecca was six years old, she asked me one of the most difficult questions known to Man. It was a quiet day and we were drifting off the white-sand beaches of Lido Key, casting jigs for bluefish, mackerel, jacks and ladyfish. As Rebecca reeled her line in she looked up from the water and asked, "Daddy, where did sin come from?"

This is a brutal question all major world religions struggle to explain. Why do people do bad things? When I was in college I spent many painful years wandering through the empty corridors of Buddhism, Hinduism, Daoism and other assorted mystical faiths. I even went on a journey to India and Nepal and got to see and touch their gods.

After drifting for years on a barren, windless sea, I discovered that an ancient book offers the only satisfying explanation to the question of evil. Believe it or not, the first book of the Bible, Genesis, sheds light on the origins of sin and evil. It's a simple yet profound story and the more I reflected on it, the clearer it became. To understand sin, and the consequences of sin, you need to go back in time to the beginning. That's right—the Bible traces sin back to one event. Much like a rock falling into the calm waters of a pond at first light, the wave created by sin has roared across the landscape of time and creation much like the killer Tsunami of 2004 that devastated Southwest Asia. Let's journey back to the beginning and see how this world was supposed to work.

Comfort and prosperity have never enriched
the world as much as adversity has.
—BILLY GRAHAM

9

The Storm

How do men act on a sinking ship? Do they hold each other?
Do they pass around the whiskey? Do they cry?

—SEBASTIAN JUNGER

The Perfect Storm

So, what's it really like being a charter captain? Why don't you step onboard the *Rainmaker IV* and join me for a typical, August day. Let me warn you, since I don't work with a first mate, I might have to put you to work setting lines.

The morning charter left the dock at 6:00. and was quite uneventful. Pleasant clients enjoyed calm seas and enough action kept everyone happy. After returning to port around 11:00 a.m. I cleaned the catch, said farewell to the guys and began preparing the boat for the next group.

I had just finished scrubbing the boat around noon and was hoping for a brief moment of silence when several cars raced to a stop at the head of the pier. By the sound of the slamming car doors and enthusiastic conversation, it was obvious these guys didn't get out of the house much. The first two men tromped down the dock, carrying a cooler—and what a cooler it was. You've seen these coolers before: Two people can sit on one, and you still have room for a third. As I loaded it on the boat I couldn't help but notice how heavy it was. So I looked inside and sure enough, the cooler was full of beer, with just enough room for some ice. No pops or sandwiches, just beer. This wasn't looking good.

Well, on the heels of the first cooler came two more guys and another cooler that was just as big. Since they had booked an eight-hour trip, I naturally assumed that the second cooler would be filled with food. After hauling it over the side, and possibly herniating the few discs in my back that were not already herniated by the first cooler, I opened this one, and it, too, was full of beer. Nothing but beer. With five of the guys waiting on the boat I politely inquired if they had brought anything to eat (to go along with all their beverages) and they assured me that Frank, who was parking the car, had lunch. Well, Frank eventually found a parking spot and came running down the dock with lunch tucked neatly under his arm—a bag of potato chips. It was going to be a very, very long eight-hour charter.

So, away we went. I had fished from three to five miles offshore in the morning with mediocre results. Not satisfied with the morning catch I decided to wear my Marco Polo hat and run east, way offshore and search deeper water. We set lines about seven miles out and began working deeper, farther and farther from shore.

The run to deeper water paid off in steady action with some 20-pound kings, plus the occasional steelhead, lake trout and smaller kings and coho salmon. As time passed, my six clients, five of whom could have been linebackers for the Green Bay Packers, grew louder and louder as the beer supply got lower and lower. Their stories began to take on mythical proportions and each tried to outdo the other as they described their adolescent accomplishments.

Around 3:30 that afternoon, with calm seas and clear skies over-head, my wife called me and asked if I'd heard about the line of severe thunderstorms bearing down on the lake. With very drunk and very loud customers in the background I calmly replied, "No, dear, I have not." At this point in the day I was in full survival mode. My goal was simple: just survive this charter and not lose any equipment—or clients—over the side.

I flipped on the weather radio and sure enough, a line of storms was headed our way and an advisory had been posted for the nearshore waters of southwestern Lake Michigan. The forecast said the storms wouldn't hit until after sunset, but as the sky darkened over the distant shoreline, we soon realized that the forecast was wrong, once again. This storm was moving fast so I had to make a choice. We could pick up lines and race back to port, or we could fish our way through the storm. We were just far enough away that by the time we pulled lines and ran, the storm would have passed so . . . we kept on fishing.

Summer thunderstorms frequently catch you by surprise, seemingly appearing out of nowhere. As a storm approaches, it often generates intense winds that flow out from the churning system. This day was no exception. The winds gradually increased from less than 10 knots to 15, 20, 25-plus knots. And the waves built from a gentle one-foot swell into a stiff, four-to-six-foot chop with the occasional six and seven footer thrown in for good measure. Add lots of white water on top and it was like fishing in the rinse cycle of a washing machine!

Fish become highly active as a storm approaches—and this day was no exception. We went from a steady bite every 10 minutes to non-stop action with frequent doubles and triples. As the storm intensified I could not get the lines in the water fast enough and the guys were having a ball hauling in big fish! Between netting fish, setting lines and controlling the boat in the building seas, I had my hands full. (Would you mind netting that fish?)

As fate would have it, this storm scored a direct hit and life got very interesting! With the wind roaring (literally), the tops of the waves began ripping across the surface and crashing across the transom of the boat. To keep the boat on a straight line I was forced to start the second engine (we normally troll on one engine) and alter our heading to quarter into the heavy seas.

Have you ever been *miles* from shore with a severe thunderstorm directly overhead? You'll know you're in the eye of the storm when the lightning flashes and the thunder BOOMS at the exact same time—almost as if the lightning is exploding in your face.

Rain doesn't fall from these storms when you're miles from the shore. It travels horizontally and stings your skin like thousands of tiny bullets. Standing on the back of the boat, netting fish and untangling lines (we were still fishing!) I felt as if we were coming under enemy attack. While I've never been in the military, I would imagine that a battlefield might have a similar feel.

What about our six macho anglers—the guys who, a few hours earlier, were reliving their heroic stories? Well, that was a rather interesting experience. While one of them was glued to the stern, reeling in the fish that never stopped biting, the other five were huddled as far forward on the deck as they could get. They were as quiet as mice, and if I was not mistaken, there was a look of terror in their eyes. I was rather enjoying the *silence*.

Like all summer storms, this one passed. While the front side of a storm is full of noise and fury, the backside is calm and peaceful, almost like passing through the eye of a hurricane. As the towering thunderheads moved off to the east, the wind died down and the lake lost its edge. The rain lost its sting and eventually ceased. As the sun emerged in the west, it transformed the sky from shades of purple to magenta to pink to blue. As a storm approaches, lightning rips across the heavens and the thunder roars like a lion attacking its prey. On the backside the lightning gently flickers across the tops of the thunderheads and the thunder is just a distant echo.

Clients? What happened next was quite amazing. Before the storm, they were the toughest guys on the planet. After the wind and waves subsided, their boasting, just like the thunder, was a distant echo as each of our heroes grabbed their cell phone, removed themselves as far from the others as they possibly could on a 34-foot boat and made a cell phone call that went something like this: "Hi honey, I'm OK . . . you should see the storm I just went through! I thought I was going to die . . . I love you and can't wait to see you!"

Funny how a good storm and a few waves can make a man contemplate his own mortality and the things that matter most in life. Making my living on the water, I have experienced my fair share of storms, in my boat—and in life. Physical, emotional and relational storms have wreaked havoc in my marriage, my career and my health. As painful as they were, they forced me to think about the course my life had taken. Life's storms, like nature's, vary in intensity and often arise when least expected. Some look rather ominous as they darken the horizon but fizzle upon arrival. Others appear weak from a distance but intensify as they approach and at times, these unexpected storms can ravage the landscape of our lives much like a level-5 hurricane.

One day, long, long ago a storm of unimaginable power and intensity hit the world. This storm looked harmless from a distance, but as it developed, it caused catastrophic damage that ravaged the landscape of time and forever altered the human experience. To help us understand this ancient storm and how it complicates our lives today, we need to first ask the question that my son Ethan asked one night before bed. We were talking about God, life and other deep issues 10-year-old boys ponder before bed when he asked, "Dad, why did God even create people?" Wow! Where do these questions come from and why is it that they always come out right before bed? By this time in the day my mind is ready to shut down. But kids? They want to download the day's events and tour the galaxy with random thoughts and questions.

So, let's ponder, why did God create us? Was he bored and in need of some amusement, like a person who puts a bunch of hamsters in a cage just to watch their silly antics? Or, maybe God just wanted someone to keep the world in order while he was attending to more important matters. To me, those explanations don't make much sense. It's hard to imagine God merely as some bored Artist, sitting on a star, finding his amusement in the victories and tragedies of our world. Is it possible that God created us simply because he likes us and enjoys being with us and watching us grow? After all, the Bible refers to God as our *Father,* and what father doesn't want to have a good relationship with his children?

I don't pretend for an instant to fully understand *who* God is, but I must confess, having children of my own has greatly enlarged my view and understanding of him. My wife and I have four children and we want to connect with them spiritually, emotionally and experientially. We have a relationship with them. Unlike God, my wife and I are not perfect, but we try our best as we work through the various needs, passions, joys and struggles that are a part of any family.

What does my family have to do with God, or the human race? I think the Keatings, like most individual families, are a microcosm of the whole human family: a tapestry of connections between mom and dad, children, and brothers and sisters that extend outward and that weave the human race together. Sociologists call this the "small world theory," suggesting that a mere six layers or degrees of relationships connect you to the rest of humanity.

Guess what? That's how God designed us. We are relational creatures, wired to connect with God, each other and our world through a myriad of healthy, interlocking connections. Ultimately, the human experience is really about friendships and relationships.

But why is it so difficult to maintain these ties? Why do we struggle to find God, let alone get to know God?

Let's journey back in time to when God first created this world and see if we can learn anything that will help us deal with these challenges.

In the Beginning

In the beginning, God splashed light and water across the canvas of creation and filled the world with a whole bunch of really cool plants, animals, birds and fish. Towards the end of God's creative process, the sixth day, he created the first human, Adam, and he breathed life into his soul. But, Adam was alone, so God gave him a perfect and most excellent companion named Eve.

God created Adam and Eve to be perfect. And they were naked, yet not ashamed. Can you imagine having a perfect mind and body? Can you imagine having a perfect mate? God created Adam and Eve physically and psychologically perfect. He placed them in an exciting outdoor setting that any outdoorsman would find pretty cool, and gave Adam the task of caring for his creation. Everything was perfect and Adam walked in complete and unbroken peace with God, his wife Eve, and all creation.

Adam and Eve were the crowning work of God's creative Earth project. While evolutionists suggest that humans are nothing more than evolved apes that got lucky one day when Aunt Lucy's genes accidentally mutated, the Bible says that we are different from other creatures and are created in the "Image of God." This state-of-the-art design included an advanced feature that we can think of as an internal GPS, a "God Positioning System." God hardwired this highly relational system into Adam to help him (and us) connect with God, each other and the landscape.

God also created Adam with the gift of free will. Remember, God wanted friendship; not a colony of cyborgs. In God's infinite love he knows that a real relationship requires choice. Don't you prefer knowing that your wife or girlfriend really loves you and WANTS to be with you? If you think about it, you probably wouldn't be satisfied with a mate that stayed with you because she HAD to, would you? God could have designed us as worshipping robots, but he loved us, so he gave us the freedom to choose! Sadly, freedom to choose means freedom to choose the wrong thing.

God gave Adam tremendous freedom, a perfect mate and a really awesome place to live and work. God loved Adam and Eve and wanted the best for them so he warned them about the danger of eating from a forbidden tree. "And the Lord God commanded the man, saying, 'you may surely eat of every tree of the garden, but of the tree of the knowledge of good and evil you shall not eat, for in the day that you eat of it you shall surely die'" (Genesis 2:16-17).

This was not advice given from one buddy to another. It was not a helpful suggestion. It was a warning, given from a perfect, holy God. This warning promised dire consequences. Have you ever been on the ocean or a large lake when gale warnings are flying? These weather systems produce massive, treacherous waves and often spawn squalls that race across the angry seas. Lightning, thunder and hail breach the heavens as the howling winds turn the water's surface into a confused and deadly sea. What is your response to storm warnings? A warning tells you that danger lies ahead. If you head offshore in a small boat under these conditions, you put your life at risk.

So, what was Adam thinking? Here he was . . . the premier model . . . fresh off the assembly line of life . . . the first man! All of creation was Adam's for the taking—except one fruit! How hard was that, Adam? Let the adventure begin!

Rather than taking the scenic route, they hung around the forbidden tree. One day Satan, disguised as a serpent, approached Eve and asked her a simple question, "Did God actually say you shall not eat of any tree in the garden" (Genesis 3:1)? Eve had a short conversation with the creature that the Bible describes as "crafty," and before you know it, doubt and temptation arose in her heart. Prior to this encounter, Eve lived in innocence and she trusted God. But with the serpent's encouragement, she believed Satan's lie that ignoring God wouldn't lead to death but would actually make them like God . . . so she ate the forbidden fruit. Then she gave some to her husband. Their chance to sail through eternity in perfection ended when they disobeyed God.

If we had instant replay of the Garden of Eden, we would all be sitting on the edges of our couches yelling, "What are you doing? Are you nuts? You're going to ruin a good thing! Run away from that tree!" The world was a lush, perfect, garden paradise containing four pristine rivers. As Erwin McMannus said in his book, *The Barbarian Way,* why didn't Adam build a raft, make a love boat and sail down one of the rivers and explore the newly created world with Eve? (Of course, with a rod and reel in hand!)

Are you tracking? Adam and Eve were given a clear, direct warning from their Creator: Do not eat the forbidden fruit! Obviously, they did not completely trust God. They second-guessed him, wondering if he really had their best interests at heart. They focused on the one area that was off-limits and eventually crossed a line, violating God's command when they ate the forbidden fruit. They exercised their free will and committed treason when they rebelled against God. When Adam and Eve chose to disobey God they left the protective sanctuary of God's harbor and headed offshore into the uncharted and stormy seas of sin and rebellion.

This historical and profoundly significant event is known as "Original Sin," or the "Fall of Man." For Adam, and for all who would follow in his footsteps, life was now marked by pain, suffering and death (Genesis 3:15-19). He and Eve were banished from the Garden of Eden and their relationship with God was broken. Not only were they separated from God, but their marriage was now tainted by strife, dissatisfaction and mistrust. Even Adam's job working the land got a lot harder for now he would struggle against "thorns and thistles."

Adam's treason also led to death. If you read Genesis 2:17 closely you will notice that Adam did not have to die, "*If* you eat its fruit, you are sure to die" (NLT, emphasis added). If Adam had lived in obedience to God, death (physical and spiritual) would not be a part of our world. It was through Adam's disobedience that death entered the human landscape. "Therefore, just as sin came into the world through one man, and death through sin, and so death spread to all men because all sinned" (Romans 5:12).

We Are a Race of Rebels

We are a race of rebels, born with this natural tendency to distrust God. Regardless of your age, ethnicity or social background, you are entangled in Adam's sin, "For all have sinned and fall short of the glory of God" (Romans 3:23). Our relationships with family, friends and co-workers are less than perfect, and sometimes downright miserable. Our marriages are often strained and filled with tension, disappointment and heartache. Even our work is affected by sin as many of us spend our days dreaming about what we *could* be doing or struggling with little recognition or reward.

We are created for relationship and the world is designed to operate through a network of healthy, interlocking relationships. Sin separates us from God and distorts the relationships of our world. Spiritually, emotionally and physically we all miss the mark and fall short of what *we could be*.

Much like the oil spilled from the Exxon Valdez polluted Prince William Sound in Alaska, this first sin contaminated all of God's good creation. The oil slick created by the Valdez spread across all layers of a pristine Alaskan Bay and tainted the land, sea and sky. From tiny plankton, to fish, to birds and seals and bears at the top of the food chain, life was polluted. Sadly, the corrosive effects of sin have spread to every corner of creation . . . even the outdoors we're so in love with . . . sin polluted EVERYTHING! "Cursed is the ground . . . thorns and thistles it shall bring forth" (Genesis 3:17-18).

We are traveling through uncharted seas and storms are brewing on the horizon. Adam was the first man to look into an approaching storm and underestimate what it would cost him not to follow God. Today, Satan's ancient questions echo through our lives: Is God good? Does he have your best interest at heart? Do you trust him? Sin often looks harmless from a distance but have you considered how it affects you, and the relationships of your life? Have you considered what it costs you to ignore God? Have you overestimated your abilities to navigate the storms of life?

I don't know about you, but I've done a lot of lousy things. I've *thrown* hurtful words at the most important people in my life, mistreated friends and family, abused my mind and body and have doubted God and ignored his leadership in my life. Yes, I am fatally flawed and the damage is extensive. But there is hope! Our sin has made an awful mess of this world, but that's only the first part of the Bible's story. The rest of the book is about God's grace! He's in the process of rescuing a broken world, restoring his image in humanity. Our sinfulness makes God's grace all the more amazing!

You know, sin, storms and fishing, have been a part of the human experience for a long time. Like Peter, I have spent long hours on the water. I love the feel of the wind on my face and the touch of the sun on my skin, and I still get excited with every strike. But like Peter, I was lost. My life resembled a snarled, back-lashed reel. Despite my professional success as an angler I was slowly drowning in the bad choices, broken relationships and the disappointments of my journey.

Like Peter, I was in need of a miraculous catch of fish. That's what makes God's grace so amazing. He doesn't give up on us. He knows we're lost, loves us anyway, and then comes to find us. He met Peter on the deck of his boat, he met me on mine, and he seeks you out wherever you are in your journey. Turn the page with me and allow me to share a few storms, and a few great catches from my life.

> *We are ruined by the effects of sin; we see our*
> *brokenness in every aspect of created order.*
> —SCOTT MCMINN
> *Why Sin Matters*

10

Listening to Your Life

*Listen to your life. See it for the fathomless
mystery that it is. In the boredom and pain of
it no less than in the excitement and gladness:
touch, taste, smell your way to the holy
and hidden heart of it because in the last
analysis all moments are key moments,
and life itself is grace.*

—Frederick Buechner

Now and Then: A Memoir of Vocation

The story of Peter's encounter with Jesus reminds me that being especially clear about fishing, and clear about God, can make a real difference in your life—and the lives of those around you. I don't know anything about you or where you are at with God, but let me ask you a question: *Do you think it is possible that a person could be kind and compassionate, attend church, read the Bible, pray, have a good reputation and still miss a relationship with God?*

Peter often heard Jesus warn people of the danger, of being close, but not close enough. We'll hear more about what Jesus had to say about this at the end of the chapter. But first, let me tell you how being close, but not close enough, worked for me one year at the prestigious Bob Uecker Great Lakes Fishing Invitational. This two-day tournament attracts some of the best fishermen on the Great Lakes. The rules allow teams to catch 15 fish per day. Scoring is based on 10 points per fish and 1 point per pound. Weights are rounded off to the nearest one-hundredth of a pound.

This particular year, the fishing was tough. Popular consensus was, catch 15 fish both days and you would win. Our strategy was to target a mixed-bag of coho, lakers and steelhead, since big kings were scarce. After two long days it looked like our plan paid off, we caught our limit each day. With only minutes till the weigh-in closed, we were confidently sitting in first place. As I was contemplating how to spend my share of the fat purse, one of my buddies ran over to tell me that we had just been knocked out of first place! But then he told me how close it was. We lost by less than half an ounce! My heart sank.

If you're going to beat me, then please crush me! Don't beat me by such a tiny margin! It's hard to believe that such a slight difference could stand between 30 fish after two days of fishing. But once the results were tabulated, less than half an ounce stood between first and second place. That half-ounce cost every member on my team thousands of dollars. We were so close, but the truth is, we might as well have been 29 fish and 100 pounds short at that point. That half-ounce didn't move us any closer to first. The winning team didn't look at us and offer to share their prize money because we were so close.

Do you think the same could be possible with God? You may *feel* close to God, like you've been hanging around the neighborhood with God. Doing all sorts of religious things? But in reality you may be an ocean away from God?

I was raised to know who God was, but when I became an adult, this knowledge didn't mean anything. In fact, I spent much of my life running from God. But in the midst of my struggles and doubts, God used a few storms, a great catch of fish and a traveler from a distant land to speak into my life. It was the summer of 1994 and I was the owner and operator of one the most successful and busiest charter boats on the Great Lakes. As the fish count was piling up and the cash register popping, an Australian named Mr. John Lillyman stepped onto the deck of my boat. His group had a great time and caught loads of fish, but he did something very unusual after his trip. He sent me a letter. This is what he wrote:

12 July, 1994

Dear Dan,

Once again Peter and I enjoyed a great time out fishing with you. How I wish some of my friends who fish "down under" could visit and go out with you. You have certainly proven yourself a master in this field. As I reflected on our time, I realized that it may be quite a while until I see you again and with this in mind I thought I would drop you a small note. I write not to point the finger at you in condemnation but as one traveler to another. As one who has found something I believe you need. As I talked with you the other day I saw a man with great ability and skill, but with a hole in his life. Like trolling with the engine shut down and the steering frozen, is a life without a dynamic relationship with God. Skirting around Christianity without ever making Christ the president of your life and affairs is like attempting to fish in a limping and handicapped boat. It is powerless, directionless and frustrating and ends in disaster.

I don't know exactly where you are at but I have tasted of life without Christ to know that if you are there, it is a wilderness that tears at your flesh with every year of life. God loves you. His only desire is for you to turn and come home.

He has so much for you if you will be sold out to him. Half measures are like keeping one foot on the wharf whilst the boat pulls away. It will rip you in two. Have you ever turned from yourself to give your all to Jesus Christ? I believe that God is calling you today. He waits.

Your friend,
John Lillyman

When I received this letter, I was not only offended, I was annoyed and irritated! Who was this guy with the funny accent to tell me that my life was incomplete and that I needed a *relationship* with God! After all, I was a Christian, wasn't I? As a child I went to church almost every Sunday and even attended a Christian high school. And since my parents were going to heaven, wouldn't that save me?

I was so angry that I threw the letter away one morning before leaving for the boat. But something was gnawing at me. The next day, I pulled John's letter out of the garbage and re-read it—and threw it away again. This cycle continued for several weeks, but my heart was aching and I couldn't ignore the implication. Was I fishing my way through life without any steering? Was I *dead in the water* just waiting for the next rogue wave to capsize me?

Danger Ahead!

All of us are on a journey called life. My journey began on the south side of Chicago and led me to the quiet community of Wheaton, Illinois, then Pittsburgh, Pennsylvania (where I became a Steeler fan!), and back to Wheaton. My parents' home was a safe harbor where my life found a secure mooring, but like all boats that remain tied up at the dock, I hadn't been tested. After graduating from high school in 1981, I sailed out onto the open waters of a turbulent culture and encountered cross currents and storms that I wasn't prepared for.

Having absolutely no idea what to do with my life, I decided to attend a small liberal arts college in Wenham, Massachusetts. This was a big deal as, other than camp, I had never been away from home. I hitched a ride to school with a family friend and when I stepped out of his car, my life changed forever—I discovered drinking, drugs and girls. I had always viewed the world through black and white lenses but during my time at Gordon College I discovered that my orderly, black and white world was full of gray. As my horizons expanded and as freedom and temptations confronted me, my world began to fall apart. I didn't know how to handle the contradictions within myself or in those around me. As the confusion darkened my mind, I began to rebel against the voices of authority in my life. I had no compass to lead me through this maze of freedom and choices.

Even though I was having way too much fun in college, I dropped out after the second trimester. I returned to the Midwest and began working a variety of jobs but was restless. I loved fishing and decided to start a charter fishing business on Lake Michigan. Despite a deteriorating relationship with my parents, Dad let me use our 23-foot Mako (*Rainmaker II*) to run charters. I quickly discovered that I could catch more and bigger fish faster than my competition, and within two years I built a thriving business. As my business grew, I became obsessed with catching the most fish. I found my identity in being the best. Nothing else mattered!

No Compass

By the standards of the world I looked like a huge success, but inside, I was dying. Despite the professional and monetary achievements, I was empty. At the end of every day I used to think, *Surely there must be more to life than this.* My mind was marred by deep insecurities that stemmed from being a middle child sandwiched between two very talented sisters. One was smashing records every time she got into the pool and the other was academically off the charts. Me? Stuck in the middle with average grades, trapped on the bench in basketball, and a failure at football and swimming. Low self-esteem seeped into every ounce of my being. No matter what I did at home, in school, in sports or in relationships I never felt *good enough*. Why would anyone, let alone God, care about me? The idea of a loving God was absurd! I rejected God and the faith of my parents. I began a long and dangerous search for significance and meaning, bravely setting out into the deep waters of life to chart my own course. But there was one problem; I didn't have a map or compass to guide me.

The charter business allowed me to build a unique life. Spring, summer and fall, I threw myself into work full throttle—15 hours a day, seven days a week. It was a rush and I loved the daily battle pitting me against the weather and the fish. The busy charter schedule gave my life structure during the April to October fishing season, but when the boat was put away and winter descended, my highly structured world fell apart and I would sink deeper and deeper into a void of darkness and depression. As the seasons changed I jumped from one wave crest to the next and struggled through troughs filled with inappropriate relationships and wild mood swings; from intense energy to anger to an emptiness that crippled my mind and body. I filled the darkness with sex, drugs and alcohol. While the desires of this world seemed appealing, they only deadened my pain.

After years of running, I ran into a fog bank of depression and anger. When a heavy fog settles onto the shoreline, boats without navigational aids are confined to port. Wise captains know that radar, GPS and sonar give them the freedom to venture out into the fog with confidence. I was equipped with neither and eventually lost my bearings and could no longer see the shoreline, let alone the harbor. I realized I was no longer in control of my life. The thought of abandoning ship and throwing myself into the raging seas kept creeping into my mind.

Man Overboard

Heavy seas are a part of my world and charter boats in my home state are required to keep a life ring and rope on deck. The August afternoon I lost a client over the side in heavy seas, I reached for that rescue ring without thinking. We were trolling a northeast course just outside the wreck of the SS *Wisconsin* in 132 feet of water, quartering into a heavy sea when suddenly one of my clients cried out, "Man overboard!" Isn't that what they say in the movies? In all my years as a captain, I'd never heard those words on *my* boat. I quickly looked in the direction he was staring. All I saw were the bottom of two shoes going over the side.

Instinctively I took the boat out of gear and ran to the back deck, rescue ring in hand. It was almost impossible to spot the man's head in the waves . . . but after what seemed to be an eternity, I located him (he'd passed out and then fallen) and sent the ring and rope flying. The second throw reached him. If it were not for the attached rope, I don't know if we would have gotten him back to the boat.

Have you ever rescued a drowning person in heavy seas? Do you know how hard it is to spot someone's head in 4- to 6-foot waves covered with white caps, let alone throw a rescue ring to them into the wind from the deck of a pitching and rolling boat?

When I was drowning, God reached out to me over a five-year period through four relationships and three events.

The Most Beautiful Life Ring

I was fighting for life in the heavy seas of depression when God graciously threw the first (and most beautiful) life ring to me. Her name was Mary, and we met, of all places, on my boat. Her dad and brother were regular customers, but Mary never went on the *guys* fishing trips . . . until June 26, 1989. To be honest, this charter got off to a rough start. The Pudaite's were more than an hour late and by the time Mary found her sunglasses and we left port, the best fishing of the day was over. I was ticked off! Despite my lousy attitude, I couldn't take my eyes off Mary! I really enjoyed talking with her as we fished. Before you knew it, we made a fine catch of 14 lake trout, a steelhead and a coho salmon. But it was the heavy thunderstorm at the end of the morning that sealed our fate together.

We returned to port and as I began to clean the fish, the skies rapidly darkened and a heavy storm descended on us. With thunder crashing and lightning splitting the heavens, the rest of Mary's family retreated to the car. Not Mary. She stood out in the pouring, monsoonal rain and helped rinse and bag the filets. By the time we finished, she was soaking wet. I always keep extra clothes on the boat so I lent

Mary a sweatshirt and sweat pants. Even though they were way too big, they were dry. And even though I was engaged at the time, I had to have at least one date with this brave, beautiful dark-skinned girl to get my clothes back.

Disaster Date

At this point in the story, Mary and I were attracted to each other, as in boy meets girl, boy kisses girl . . . but our first date was a disaster. I wasn't just late, I was a no show! I was so tired from chartering that I slept through our *first date* on the living room floor at my parents' house! Mary had to leave the next day for a work-related trip to India and I, the great fisherman, did not make a good impression. Somehow we survived the rough start and our two lives began a journey into the unknown.

When Mary returned from India we spent countless hours sipping coffee at Periwinkles Café, late summer nights hanging out in Chicago (me with little or no sleep), having long conversations talking about everything and nothing at all, or just being together. At that point in my life I was highly destructive and women were merely objects to be conquered and tossed aside. But, my relationship with Mary was very different. She was a great listener, asked challenging questions and she reached out across the darkness to me. I couldn't push her away and God protected us from my dysfunctional tendencies.

Over the next six years we became more than best friends, we became soul mates. Just as Mary stood by me in the driving rain, she stood by me during some of my darkest days as I battled depression from 1989 to 1994. As I struggled with darkness and rage, Mary was the one person who demonstrated what real love looked like. Many years later I asked her why she stuck with me. She said it was God's love working through her. Today, we can see God's love reflecting back at us through our four children.

The Deadly Screwdriver

Fast-forward to 1992 when I discovered that a screwdriver should be classified as a deadly weapon. In 1989 I was diagnosed as bi-polar manic-depressive, underwent extensive psychotherapy and relied on medication to cope. Winters were tough and at times I would get so depressed that I wanted to end my life. When I was younger I tried to take my own life several times, once with pills and once with a knife, but I couldn't do it. Now, I was on a downward spiral and, one afternoon, my anger brought me millimeters from death.

A symptom of my disease was losing my temper when things didn't work out exactly the way I wanted them to. I got easily frustrated and could go from zero to full-blown rage in a matter of seconds. This afternoon I was assembling a computer table, and it just wasn't going well, and of course, it was everyone else's fault. The directions weren't easy enough to follow; the pieces weren't cut to fit together right. Everyone but me and my basic ineptness with tools was to blame. Finally, my aggravation with a stubborn crossbeam spilled over into a careless act of rage. Easily frustrated when working with tools, I made a nearly deadly mistake. Curled up under the table, I couldn't push a crossbeam into place. Instead of taking the time to see why it was stuck I tried to force it with a hammer and screwdriver. Still lying on my side, I placed the tip of the screwdriver against the beam in such a way that the tip was pointing right at me, then angrily blasted its butt with my hammer. Whack! The tip bounced off the crossbeam and shot directly into my right eye, piercing it. Time froze, and everything went dark.

LISTENING TO YOUR LIFE   115

I pulled myself out from under the table and was flooded with the conscious realization that I had just maimed myself. I ran to the bathroom, blood spurting everywhere—I was blind in one eye! I lived on the ground floor of a three story apartment building. I remembered the landlord's girlfriend had a business on the third floor so I bolted up three flights of stairs and banged on the door. She opened the door and, amidst the gasps, rushed me to her car. At the time I lived on the near west side of Chicago and she was headed to Northwestern Hospital. After about three blocks she looked at me and said, "you're not going to make it!" So she turned around and headed to St. Mary's Hospital, which was very close!

At the hospital Doctor Beltran saved my eye but she told me I was lucky to be alive. The screwdriver stopped three millimeters short of my brain. This accident really shook me up. My anger almost had cost me my life. Despite my struggles with depression and darkness, I now realized how desperately I wanted to live. Why did God spare my life?

My Asian Adventure

God's pursuit escalated in 1994 when he led me to take a trip to Asia, an adventure that stretched me beyond anything I had ever experienced. I traveled the diverse and dusty roads of the Hindu nation India, went into the hills of the Buddhist Kingdom of Nepal and spent a month in the Muslim Maldives Islands. This was not your typical tourist outing. My friends were from India and Nepal and they took me off the beaten path. At one point I was even imprisoned by the Garhwal Rifles light infantry brigade in the remote hills of Manipur, India. This story deserves a book of its own, but let me tell you, I never felt more powerless in my life!

The timing of this trip was amazing and could only have been orchestrated by the hand of God. In my thirst for meaning and truth, I had studied eastern religions and the occult but this trip immersed me in the cultures of the East. I saw and touched the gods that I had read about. I walked in their temples and saw people of immense poverty crying out to objects made of stone and clay, begging for mercy. But *who* would answer those calls, for "their idols are like scarecrows in a cucumber field, and they cannot speak; they have to be carried, for they cannot walk. Do not be afraid of them, for they cannot do evil, neither is it in them to do good" (Jeremiah 10:5). The poverty and the disregard for life in India opened my eyes to levels of suffering I never could have imagined. I witnessed first hand how terribly the people of these lands treated one another. Hinduism, Buddhism and Islam were not the answer. I returned to America a changed man with more questions than answers. Looking back, I see how God led me to India but did not abandon me there. I saw with my eyes, smelled with my nose, heard with my ears and touched with my hands what sin, hatred, and evil were doing to people.

Australian Stealth Bomber

The spring of 1994 found me consumed by another busy year on the boat. What is so amazing about God is that he knows right where you are and he seeks you in the midst of your journey, just like he sought Peter on the Sea of Galilee. In the height of my summer season God sent a B2 Stealth Bomber into my life—the Australian letter writer John Lillyman. At this point my life was a blur. Fish were hitting the deck, the cash register was singing, and I was winning tournaments. But I still was walking with a spiritual limp.

That's when the Lord gave John the courage to send the letter. As my anger at him settled, I began to contemplate his message. Finally, I sought him out and asked a few, well, a whole lot of questions over coffee at the Stupe, a campus café at Wheaton College. John became my friend and mentor and he walked with me as I wrestled with God, and my life struggles. Today, we are still bound by a friendship that is deeper than ourselves.

Crazy Jim and the Big Catch

I also sought out another friend that God had put in my life years earlier, Jim Flickinger. Jim was the lifeline that God used to pull me back to his lifeboat. We had built a unique friendship 10 years earlier, which began with one of those really memorable fishing trips. In the fall of 1983, a mutual friend, Doc Rupprecht, had invited both of us to go casting for staging Chinook salmon in the harbor at Kenosha, Wisconsin. During the 1980s Kenosha received a huge run of these kings and at times it seemed like you could walk across the water on fish!

We converged on the harbor toward sundown, Jim with a Dunkin' Donuts coffee in hand, and me with a huge supply of pearl M2 Flatfish, the weapon of choice. With light winds and balmy temperatures, Doc launched his 16-foot, blue-hulled boat and away we went. With the World Series blaring in the background we experienced a night filled with the sounds of kings rolling on the surface, smashing strikes, singing drags and great conversation and laughter—this is what God made us for! Doc's fish box was useless for this haul and by the time we quit, the deck of his boat was covered with ginormous kings. With a catch like this, I should have known God was up to something.

Like Mary and John, Jim extended the hand of grace and camaraderie to me. That night we forged a friendship that continues today. We've shared many great adventures on the water, like the morning of his wedding day when the groom's party went fishing and caught 39 salmon!

Jim was journeying through life with God, but like Peter, he didn't fit my stereotypical definition of what a Christian looked like. He was a good man, but once in a while he *stubbed his toe*, like the time we ventured into a biker bar late one night. Jim was super articulate and he sometimes made sharp comments that would rattle people. This night he rattled the very large and scary looking bikers at the end of the bar. But before they could kill Jim (who happens to be tiny!) he talked his way out of trouble and before long the guys were buying us drinks! Jim was always very open about his love for the Lord, but he was equally honest about his humanity and the sins and shortcomings that were a nearly constant struggle for him. I sought Jim's guidance, sometimes over a nice single malt scotch or a beer, and learned much about God, friendship and myself.

Eventually, Jim invited me to church late in the summer of 1994. I had steered clear of the church since high school, but I accepted his invitation. After all, I never thought I would have to *go to church* since I was a highly sought charter captain and Sundays were busy days. But once again the hand of God interfered with my world and, Sunday after Sunday, the wind howled out of the northeast. Huge waves made the lake too rough to fish. I found myself sitting in church, grappling with Pastor John Casey's sermons, pondering God, life, and wondering if there was a connection between God and me. After all, Jesus pursued Peter on the Sea of Galilee, where he calmed the seas during a raging storm. Did he create the waves on Lake Michigan to drive me to him, "[He] stirs up the sea so that its waves roar . . ." (Jeremiah 31:35).

My Wrestling Match

With the '94 fishing season winding down, I began to wrestle with God and I cried out to him in my pain and said, "If you are real, then reveal yourself to me!" Like the day I had a screwdriver in my eye and cried out for sight, I wanted eyes to see him and a heart to believe in him. With an autumn explosion of colors painting the landscape, I would rise early in the mornings, read my Bible and go for long walks on DuPage County's Prairie Path. It was on those walks that I truly met Jesus. For the first time I was still and I heard God's quiet voice and I surrendered my life to him.

After so many years of running, I was ready to listen to the voice of the One who hung each of the billions of stars perfectly in the night sky. For years I had been looking for meaning in the things of this world rather than in the Creator of this world. I thought God was nothing more than a distant, angry being who created the earth, spun it into existence and then abandoned us. I didn't think he cared about the struggles of a man like me. But through the trials of my journey, I discovered that God was neither distant nor angry. He was much closer than I ever imagined, and he had been pursuing me even though I was running from him. I understood that God is alive and he is holy and he loves me—but he wasn't going to settle for half of me. God had been saying, *Dan, I want all of you.* In other words, I had to come to God on his terms and respond to his call.

After years of struggling, I slowly began to understand that I could never fill the emptiness or remove the pain on my own. "Self-medicating" the ache with alcohol, drugs or inappropriate relationships only made matters worse. Like Peter, I realized just how ugly my sin was. But for the first time, I realized just how big God was. For the first time, I realized I was not alone with that sin. I discovered that Jesus came into the world to restore my relationship with him. He does this by taking away my sins and giving me a new life.

What's the Big Deal?

At this point you might be thinking what's the big deal? I've only broken a few rules. Can't we just say we're sorry, do a few good deeds and make restitution for our mistakes? That's what I thought. But the truth is, an impassable ocean separates us from God. No matter how good we are we cannot cross these violent and stormy waters.

The world is full of people who have tried to swim across this stormy ocean through acts of kindness, good deeds, or religious gymnastics, but religiosity will eventually fail, "For by works of the law no human being will be justified in his sight" (Romans 3:20). Or, as *The Message* puts it, "We are all sinners in a sinking boat."

In other words, the odds of you connecting with God *on your own* are not quite as good as your chances of swimming across the North Atlantic during a level-5 hurricane. For just a moment, stand on the coast and look at the 30-foot waves crashing against the rocks below. Imagine what the waves would look like offshore, as 150-mile-per-hour winds turn the open sea into an absolute nightmare of chaos. With water temperatures in the low 50s you, wearing only your speedo and a pair of goggles, decide to go for it, and you throw yourself into the raging surf. Let's pretend you are not smashed to a pulp against the rocks and you survive the frigid water. How far will you be able to swim through the massive waves before you end as dead as a piece of driftwood?

If religion, clean living and good deeds don't restore our relationship with God, what does? Is it possible that God's book tells us the secret? After all, what book is more reliable than the Bible? The Bible says we are all separated from a perfect, Holy God by our sin. "But your iniquities have made a separation between you and your God, and your sins have hidden his face from you so that he does not hear" (Isaiah 59:2). In *The Cross of Christ,* John Stott explains this barrier as the natural consequence of our violating God's moral law, which is an expression of his righteous character.

The same Creator who left his fingerprints on the mountains, sea and heavens also wrote his law on our hearts, "there is something deep within [us] that echoes God's yes and no, right and wrong" (Romans 2:15 MSG). We have this internal sense of right and wrong and God is offended every time we mistreat him, our neighbors, our world or our own self.

Sin distorts our lives and relationships. But God's love is greater than our sin! He solved the dilemma of needing to uphold the law and punish the guilty. How? He sent Jesus Christ, the perfect God-man to stand in our place. When Jesus was nailed to the cross he took the penalty that I deserved and his sacrifice cancelled my debt. *Christ died for our sins* (1 Corinthians 15:3).

What Will You Do?

Jesus died for our sins. If you allow him to be the captain of your life, you are declared righteous or acceptable in God's sight (Romans 8:1). He wasn't obligated to save us. He doesn't owe us anything. That's what makes God's grace so amazing. He simply loves his children and sent his one and only Son into the world to rescue us and restore our relationship with him.

But it doesn't take effect until *you* make a decision of faith. Each of us has to make our own choice: Will you trust Jesus as your Savior? We'll explore how to make this radical move in the next chapter. But first let me tell you what Jesus said about being close, but not close enough. Someone once asked him if many would be saved. In response Jesus said something that sent chills through many. He said many will be greatly surprised, and disappointed one day, "A lot of you are going to assume that you'll sit down to God's salvation banquet just because you've been hanging around the neighborhood all your lives. Well, one day you're going to be banging on the door, wanting to get in, but you'll find the door locked and the Master saying, 'Sorry, you're not on my guest list'" (Luke 13:24-27 MSG).

So close, and yet so far! I learned what that felt like at the Uecker tournament. Have you ever felt that way? Guess what. According to Jesus, many will feel that way at the end of their lives. So close, and yet so far.

God used an Australian stealth bomber to write a humble letter, a beautiful life ring (who became my wife), crazy Jim, a deadly screwdriver and a few exciting twists and turns to call me away from death into life. You may think becoming a Christian was the end of my journey—that I had reached my destination—but this was only just the beginning!

Are you listening to your life? In the same way that God reached out to Peter, is it possible that God has been pursuing you through the daily joys, mysteries and struggles of your life? Has God thrown you a life ring? Are you willing to reach out amidst the waves and to take hold of his gift?

Before you cast God out of your boat, you need to check your fuel and supplies. How far can you make it? Storm clouds are forming on the horizon. In the next chapter we're going to travel alongside Peter and meet a famous soldier who was close, but not close enough. For this reason, Jesus sent a fisherman to visit him. Who knows, maybe we can learn something from this man's journey.

> *Salvation is a gift, as free as the air we breathe.*
> *It is to be obtained, like any other gift, without money*
> *and without price; there are no other terms.*
> —D. L. MOODY
> *The Overcoming Life*

11

The Big Wave

The fishermen know that the sea is dangerous and the storm terrible, but they have never found these dangers sufficient reason for remaining ashore.

—Vincent Van Gogh

I'll never forget the day. I thought my 34-foot Atlantic charter boat was going to roll over, clients aboard, miles from shore. We were fishing about 10 miles from port when an unexpected storm spawned tremendous wind. Without warning, the seas built from a 3- to 5-foot chop into towering waves that topped 10 feet. Now, guys who regularly ply salt water might think I'm being quite the weenie complaining about 10-foot waves, but these were not swells. These were some of the fastest, steepest, meanest waves I've ever encountered. Their crests were covered with angry white water and they had no backside. As the boat climbed to the peak of each wave, it fell violently to land in a narrow trough, only to rise, and fall again.

As I watched the seas build I began to wonder how my boat would handle the long run home in such extreme conditions. We were in full survival mode—but the fish were biting! The storm was on us so fast, that I had to choose between a back-breaking run, which would have taken at least an hour, or riding the waves on a slow troll heading back in. I streamlined our trolling spread and began a southwest troll toward home. No sense wasting hot fish, and trolling back to port would be a lot less brutal. But my clients were not having fun. In fact, I think they were terrified as the waves began crashing across the transom. Large waves are a thing of beauty and power and they never cease to amaze me. I was hoping the wind would back off but truth be told, things just were getting worse. The waves intensified to the point that the *Confusion*, a 36-foot Tiara trolling alongside us, began to disappear from sight as she slipped in between the waves. All we could see were the tips of her outriggers.

Finally, my clients had had enough. I reeled in our lines, netted one last fish, and braced myself for a long hellacious ride back to port. By this point the seas were running 8 to 12 feet high with the occasional whopper thrown in. The wind blew so hard that it knocked the tops off the waves, making it almost impossible to see as the boat crashed through the horizontal spray and walls of angry water. The Atlantic handled the conditions better than my clients as we cut a quartering course into the waves.

Out of nowhere came a massive rogue wave that hit us sideways on the port side! I hung onto the steering wheel as the boat rolled to starboard at an angle I've never experienced, the cockpit sole nearly vertical! My clients, huddled on the port bench, flew across the boat's beam head-first and landed in a pile. I've been on roller coasters that tip and turn and flip you around but they are designed to do this! Charter boats are not and in all my years running one, this was the first time I was rattled to my core. Never have I been aboard a boat that rolled so hard. I thought we were done!

Through the grace of God, the old girl righted herself and we made it safely back to port. Safe back in the slip, my clients had one question: How big was that wave? Were we in danger of tipping over? I honestly didn't know what to tell them, although I know we were just about as close to capsizing as I had ever been before. While it is hard to say just how big that wave was, my best guess would place it at, well, big. Really, really big. That evening as I talked with the other captains who made the long run back, they all said the same thing, "There was one giant wave that I thought was going to do us in!"

Whether you own a boat, or just like to sit on the bank and occasionally dunk a worm, we will all meet that one, last wave that's just
too big to steer around. We all have an expiration date and when you
step out towards the shores of eternity, where will you land? Will you
be close, but not close enough? Jesus says many people who assumed
they were in his Kingdom will be greatly distressed when they stand
before God. These souls will discover, only too late, that they are not
in God's Kingdom.

Our friend the apostle Peter knows a thing or two about fishing,
boats and big waves. After hanging out with Jesus for about three years,
he also learned much about being close, but not close enough. For this
reason Jesus sent him to a famous soldier, who was close, but not close
enough.

Cornelius was an officer in the Roman Army, by far the most powerful military force of his day. He wasn't just an officer; he was a com-
mander in the Italian Regiment. But he was not a typical Roman soldier. Unlike most, he feared God, gave generously to the poor, treated
his neighbors well and prayed on a regular basis. As a leader, he was
well respected by fellow Romans and the Jewish religious community.
By all accounts, you would have thought he was in the club and had
green lights all the way to heaven. But despite his most valiant efforts,
his success and good reputation, he was still not close enough.

To make a long story short, Cornelius had a vision in which an
angel told him to send for Peter, who was in a different city. Peter got a
message from God to go with the men that Cornelius had sent to fetch
him. This is in Acts 10 and is pivotal because Peter, a Jew, is learning
that all men, both Jew and Gentile (like Cornelius) are part of God's
plan for salvation.

So, Peter arrives at Cornelius house and Cornelius fell at his feet and worshipped him. Wrong move! "Peter pulled him up and said, 'None of that—I'm a man and only a man, no different from you'" (Acts 10:26 MSG). Fortunately, Cornelius had an open and teachable spirit and he invited Peter to share God's story with him and his household.

What Did Peter Tell Cornelius?

If you ever thought the Good News was boring, then you haven't heard what Peter told Cornelius. Peter began with God's love for all people—even a Roman soldier. This was radical thinking! The Roman army was feared and hated by the Jews. Many Jews may have disliked Cornelius simply because he represented the tyrannical, oppressive government that was occupying their land and placing a heavy tax burden on their shoulders. Some may even have had a friend or relative who had been killed by a Roman solder. Why did Peter take the gospel to Cornelius?

Since the dawn of time God has always done the unexpected. On this day he sent Peter against the current of popular opinion. Peter assured Cornelius that Jesus came to rescue men and women from all tribes and nations. I would have loved to been there as he excitedly shared the miracles he had personally witnessed Jesus perform. I wonder if he told the story about the time the giant waves almost sank their boat and how Jesus miraculously calmed the water. Or maybe he told them about the little girl he brought back to life. Or maybe he spoke of the lepers they all thought were as good as dead—until Jesus touched them.

Peter could have spent weeks telling his new friends about his experiences with Jesus, but he focused on the climax of the story: Jesus' execution on a Roman cross. As an officer, Cornelius undoubtedly had access to current intel and had heard of Jesus' crucifixion. He may have even been a witness. The Bible tells us that a centurion watched Jesus die and said, "Truly this man was the Son of God" (Mark 15:39)! Was it Cornelius?

Cornelius probably had heard the reports of Jesus' resurrection. This was big news! Jesus was hugely popular and his execution was not a secret. A Roman soldier even pierced his side to make sure he was dead. His lifeless body was taken down from the cross and placed in a tomb and a stone was rolled across the entrance. To secure the grave, Roman guards stood at the entrance. I am sure they thought *game over*.

But after three days, Jesus walked out of that tomb. According to the Bible the tomb was empty! As badly as the authorities wanted to kill Jesus and silence his followers, don't you suppose they set up a massive dragnet to locate the missing body? Guess what? They never found it!

Peter enthusiastically confirmed all that Cornelius had undoubtedly heard. He told Cornelius even more stunning news, that he had personally seen Jesus alive. They even shared one last fishing adventure on the Sea of Galilee. And yes, like all fishing trips with Jesus, they made a huge catch—153 fish to be exact! Jesus even prepared a final fish dinner over an open fire.

Peter had seen it all and there could be no doubt that Jesus was the real deal. If Cornelius had any doubts, all he had to do was look at the powerful, living evidence walking around in the cities and countryside. The lame that Jesus touched? They were now walking. The blind he laid hands on? Now they could see. The insane he encountered? They were now in their right minds. But a man named Lazarus may have been the strongest evidence pointing to Jesus' divinity. Lazarus died. His body had been wrapped in traditional burial cloth and placed in a tomb. For three long days his family and friends mourned his passing. But the carpenter from Nazareth showed up at the tomb and did the unexpected. He restored Lazarus to life! Lazarus was powerful evidence pointing to Jesus' divinity. In Peter's words, truly Jesus was the Anointed One of whom the prophets had spoken. He was the Messiah.

But the story doesn't end here! Peter told Cornelius that Jesus died for a purpose, that he died to rescue him and all sinners. That is the Good News of the gospel message, "There is peace with God through Jesus Christ, who is Lord of all" (Acts 10:36 NLT). This amazing offer is available to all who trust him. Those who repent will be forgiven and adopted into God's family (John 1:12).

Soldiers of Faith

Cornelius thought he was close. He thought he had been good enough to earn God's favor. But on that day he discovered that just knowing about God and trying really hard wasn't enough. His best efforts and all his good deeds did not merit God's acceptance. Once Peter explained God's rescue plan it was like a beam of bright sunlight breaking through the clouds. Everything was clear. He now understood that God was personally interested in him. But his sin separated him from a perfect, holy God and no amount of good deeds or offerings could restore his relationship with God. He now realized that Jesus' death and resurrection had made a way for him, the most unlikely of people, to connect with God.

Today was his day. He wanted a new beginning. He wanted to enlist in God's Kingdom. As an officer, Cornelius understood better than most that you couldn't just act like a soldier. You couldn't just buy a uniform and a sword and start fighting. In his own life, becoming a soldier began with a commitment to the Roman Empire. He had to embrace its identity, laws and goals. He had to surrender his old identity and submit to the masters and mission of the Empire. The very day he enlisted, the government gave him a uniform, a new identity and promised to provide for all his needs. They pledged to train and equip him to be a soldier. He was now part of a new family and he had a mission. As a soldier he was accustomed to working long hours. He knew about battle and bloodshed and that death was always a possibility.

But until he enlisted, he would always be an imposter, no matter how hard he tried to pose as a soldier. No matter how colorful his uniform or sharp his sword, he would be an outsider until he trusted the government enough to enlist, and was given a new identity in the army. Until the government recognized him as one of their soldiers, he would be a pretender.

Cornelius did not want to be an imposter with God. He now understood that Jesus was making an amazing invitation to him and his family. He also understood that to enter God's Kingdom, he must first make a commitment. He couldn't just get a religious uniform, do religious duties and try really hard. He had to be accepted into God's family on God's terms. As Peter showed him, acceptance by God had nothing to do with his own efforts. Acceptance into God's family was based solely on one man's sacrifice—and that man was Jesus Christ. All Cornelius needed to do was receive this free gift and to trust Jesus for all his needs. If he would turn toward Jesus, at that moment, Jesus would give him a new heart, a new life and a new identity. It might take a lifetime to grow that relationship, but it would begin now!

On the very day Peter visited him, Cornelius humbled himself and received God's amazing gift. For the first time in his life, he turned to God and repented and accepted Jesus Christ as his Savior. Instead of trying to earn God's forgiveness, he humbly received it and dedicated his life to him. At that very moment his sins were washed away and his name was written in the book of life (Revelation 20:12). In this moment, the fierce Roman centurion became a brother in Christ with the Jewish fisherman. They had the same master and shared a common mission. Cornelius still had much to learn on the long voyage ahead but now the warrior had peace with God.

What About Us?

Peter's encounter with Cornelius reminds us that just knowing *about* God or trying really hard, doing good deeds and living a good, honest life isn't enough. Cornelius knew some things about God and he even conducted much of his life in a godly manner. Maybe you're like Cornelius? You think you're close. But as Cornelius discovered, you might as well be a million miles away because *feeling* close doesn't bring peace between you and God.

Is God trying to make it personal with you right now? Is he bringing me, Dan the fisherman, an unlikely messenger, right into your home today? I've done my best to talk with you as if we were fishing together and I sincerely hope that Peter's story, and my journey, have brought clarity to your life. If I could, I'd look you right in the eyes and ask you what you think about all this.

Jesus said, "I am the way, the truth, and the life. No one can come to the Father except through me" (John 14:6 NLT). Eternal life is found in him alone, "I am the resurrection and the life. Whoever believes in me, though he die, yet shall he live, and everyone who lives and believes in me shall never die" (John 11:25). Listen closely to his words. The only path to achieve peace with God, and eternal life is through Jesus. That's it!

What would you do if someone at the office or in the neighborhood made the kinds of radical statements that Jesus did? In *Mere Christianity*, C. S. Lewis says, "A man who was merely a man and said the sort of things Jesus said would not be a great moral teacher. He would either be a lunatic—on a level with the man who says he is a poached egg—or else he would be the Devil of Hell. Either this man was, and is, the Son of God: or else a madman or something worse."

Lewis goes on to say, "Either Jesus is who he says he is, the Son of God, or he is a raving lunatic. You must make your choice."

What do you think?

When the nails were driven into his flesh, Jesus, the Son of God reached out to you and paid the ultimate price. He gave his life for you and me. His sacrifice on the cross washed away my sins. Would you like his blood to wash your sins away?

The same Creator who raised the mountains and filled the heavens with endless lights formed you and breathed life into your soul. Whether you admit it or not, whether you realize it or not, you bear the fingerprints of God. According to the Bible, every man, woman and child is *created in the image of God.* You were designed to live in a relationship with God and his Son made a way for you to engage with your Creator.

I believe Jesus is calling people to himself all the time. You only have three responses. You can reject Christ and his claims, or you can receive his free gift of grace, or you can say, "I'm not ready, but I want to investigate this stuff a bit."

If you are kicking the tires of Christianity, then kick away! Cry out to God and ask him to "reveal yourself to me, show me who YOU really are, don't leave me to figure it out from other people's opinions." Keep seeking and explore God's Word, the Bible. If you are not familiar with the Bible, or just want to learn more, then begin with some of its clearest parts. John 3 and Romans 3 are great for those just beginning a journey with Jesus. If you want to dig deeper, then explore John's entire gospel. But, as you read, ask Jesus to make his identity clear to you and to give you a sense of awe about his greatness.

Maybe at this moment you wonder, "Can I trust Jesus?" Truth is, even after I received Jesus as my Savior, it took me years to *trust* him. You may be surprised to know that Jesus himself wants us to wrestle with this question—who is he? He even asked his closest friends, the disciples, this same question: "Who do you say I am?" (Matthew 16:15).

Jesus wants us to be crystal clear on this. Wherever we are right now, Jesus wants to reveal himself to us. He doesn't want us to engage in a theological conversation about his deity, either. It goes much farther and deeper than intellectually agreeing that Jesus is God. It is more than just following a set of rules or instructions. Jesus wants us to respond with awe and wonder, just like Peter did when the incredible catch of fish filled his nets. He wants us to surrender our lives to him and trust him when he says, "I will never leave you or forsake you." He wants us to shout with Peter who said, "You are the Messiah, the Son of the living God" (Matthew 16:16 NLT)! In other words, he wants us to set our life coordinates on him.

If you are stuck, God can fix that. All you have to do is ask. Cry out to God. Tell him how you feel and say, "God, I know there is more to this world than I can see, but I have many questions and some difficult emotions come to the surface when I contemplate You. I don't want to follow my emotions or float along with popular opinion and cultural trends that block me from seeing you. I am open to you and ask you to reveal more of yourself to me." Escape to a quiet place in the woods or on the water and talk with God.

What Rhythm Does Your Heartbeat Follow?

If you have spent any amount of time outdoors, you can't deny that there's a natural rhythm built into the waters that sustain this planet. What about you? What rhythm does your heartbeat follow? What sustains you? What takes you from one foggy, damp Monday morning to the next? Is the pace of your life set by the standards of this world? Or, is your life calibrated to a higher standard?

God gave you a heart to enjoy the outdoors and all he created. He also planted a deeper longing in your soul—a longing for purpose and meaning; a longing to spend eternity with God. I don't know about you but this thought overwhelms me. The Creator who carved the oceans deep and who robes the majestic mountain peaks with purple glory day after day is in pursuit of my soul! The Architect, who hung each distant star perfectly in the cosmos, knows me by name and seeks to live in relationship with me. You don't ignore the passionate call of fishing. Why would you want to ignore God's call?

Maybe somebody in your life has a personal relationship with Jesus Christ. Spend a little time with this person and ask how he or she became a Christian. Explore some books or CDs or websites that reveal solid evidences for God's reality and that clarify why and how to begin a relationship with God. I've included a short list at the end of this book.

Jesus met our friend Peter on the rough and deadly waters of Galilee. Jesus didn't call him into the synagogue and make him pass a test. He met Peter on the water and extended the hand of peace to him. When Peter was confronted by the Truth embodied in Jesus, he realized his dire need of a Savior. Jesus is seeking you, my friend. He isn't going to ask any of us if we went to church. As Cornelius discovered, good deeds, clean language, and going to church don't make you a

Christian, or guarantee you a place in heaven, any more than going to fishing seminars makes you a fisherman. You have to get out on the water and spend some time fishing. You see, what really matters most is what you believe about Jesus and how you respond to his invitation. Will you accept him or reject him?

Wherever you may be, he wants you to turn to him, "Behold, I stand at the door and knock. If anyone hears my voice and opens the door; I will come in" (Revelation 3:20).

Would you like a fresh start? Would you like Jesus to do the unexpected and restore you to life? No matter how far you've run from God. No matter how many bad choices you've made, God, the Eternal Fisherman, is seeking you. In Jesus, God became man. He broke bread with us, wept with us and even went fishing with some of us. He also made an extraordinary offer to you. He offers forgiveness of your sins and eternal life.

Can you see more clearly than ever that Jesus is much greater than you ever imagined? Can you see how your sin separates you from a perfect, holy God? Are you sobered by the danger of rejecting Jesus? We all will face that one wave that is just too big to navigate. Are you prepared to meet your maker?

If you truly believe that Jesus is who he claims to be and you are ready to follow him into the only adventure that lasts forever, start with John 3:16: "For God so loved the world that he gave his only Son, that whoever believes in him should not perish but have eternal life."

1. To begin a relationship with Jesus Christ acknowledge your sin and your need of a Savior. In your heart of hearts ask Jesus to forgive you and to cleanse your heart and life.
2. Thank Jesus for taking the shame and penalty you deserved, and dying on a cross. He paid your debt.

3. Jesus defeated death—he is Alive! There is great power in his victory over death.
4. Give Jesus control of your life.
5. Ask him to help you turn from a sinful lifestyle.
6. Allow him to realign your will and desires with his perfect will.
7. Begin the journey! The gospel is all about transformation, and when you allow Jesus Christ to be Captain of your life, you will grow.

This simple prayer will sum it all up:

"Jesus, forgive me of my sins and cleanse my heart. Thank you for dying on the cross for me and paying my dept. I know you are alive, please take control of my life and turn me from a worldly, sinful lifestyle. Realign my will and desires with your perfect will."

If you've decided to embark on this great adventure, you might be wondering what to do next. Great question! In chapter 12 we will discuss some practical steps, and resources God gives us to navigate the challenges of life, and to grow as a follower of Christ. But before we get to those steps, let me assure you of one thing: What God says will happen the moment you commit your life to Jesus. When you confess with your lips and believe in your heart that Jesus is Lord, and that God raised him from the dead, you will be saved (Romans 10:9). When you die, you can rest assured that Jesus has prepared a place for you and will take you to your forever home—heaven. Jesus himself tells us that, "Truly, truly, I say to you whoever hears my word and believes him who sent me has eternal life. He does not come into judgment, but has passed from death to life" (John 5:24).

Jesus said, "The thief comes only to steal and kill and destroy. I came that they may have life and have it abundantly (John 10:10). The gospel is ultimately about transformation. When you trust Jesus and give your life to him, you become a new person. "You are not the same anymore, for the old life is gone. A new life has begun" (2 Corinthians 5:17 NLT)! You may not feel any different, or you might feel the presence of the Holy Spirit in your heart. Feelings come and feelings go, but God's Word says that the moment you prayed this simple prayer you were adopted into God's family. You now have a new identity in Christ and your sins are forgiven (Colossians 1:13-14). He will give you a new heart and frees you from the deadly power of sin (Romans 6:5-11). Freedom from sin doesn't mean you don't sin anymore. It means that when Jesus sends his Spirit to live in you, you will grow. One step at a time, he will lead you out of sinful patterns. You're still human so you will still face many struggles but Jesus promises those who trust him that, "I will never leave you or forsake you" (Hebrews 13:5).

If you just received Jesus into your life, tell someone! Peter shared his life-transforming journey with people he met and with those who live down the corridors of time. After all, you wouldn't keep that trophy fish you caught a secret, would you?

Whether it is the sight of calm water at first light, the sound of a reel's drag, the memory of yesterday's fishing trip or the anticipation of tomorrow's catch, the love of fishing reaches deep into your heart. God knows your heart intimately. He should, since he created it!

I challenge you to follow the Eternal Fisherman, Jesus Christ. Let me warn you, if you follow him, load the boat with your best gear and batten down the hatches, storm clouds are forming on the horizon. Just because you are right with God, navigating the challenges of life is not free of danger. But don't worry, your journey is secure. Jesus will lead you through the storms and into deep waters. He will fill your nets beyond anything you could imagine.

> *A man who was merely a man and said the sort of things*
> *Jesus said would not be a great moral teacher. He would*
> *either be a lunatic—on a level with the man who says he is*
> *a poached egg—or else he would be the Devil of Hell.*
> *You must make your choice. Either this man was, and is,*
> *the Son of God: or else a madman or something worse.*
>
> —C. S. Lewis
> *Mere Christianity*

12

What's Your Heading?

Believing in God is less a position than a journey, less a
realization than a relationship. It doesn't leave you cold
like believing the world is round. It stirs your blood
like believing the world is a miracle. It affects who
you are and what you do with your life like believing
your house is on fire or somebody loves you.

—FREDRICK BUECHNER

Whistling in the Dark

Daylight was still well behind the horizon as I opened my car door and had my senses filled by the muffled roaring of water crashing against rocks. It's a sound I've grown to love—and to hate. Large waves have been a part of my life, on the water and off, and this day would be no exception. Once again, my boating and fishing skills would be tested against the fury of an angry lake.

These waves were crashing just outside the small, rugged harbor in the Chicago area called Trident Marina, where I began my charter career. To be honest, Trident wasn't much. She was little more than a shallow lagoon with about 100 slips. A shallow channel cutting through a thin beach connected her to Lake Michigan. No break wall protected the channel, which usually needed dredging. When the wind howled from the northeast, east or southeast, it spawned large breakers that devoured the channel and required nerves of steel to crash through. Simply put, it was a navigational nightmare.

On this day I quickly headed down to my boat, an inboard 23-foot Mako center console—the *Rainmaker II*. She was my first charter boat. She wasn't big, but she was a perfectly balanced water rocket. She was ideal for busting through Trident's treacherous channel. She was my first love.

I had just finished setting the boat up when my clients arrived. After brief introductions I advised them that the lake was a bit rough and gave them the option of rescheduling. The thought of hurtling through a dangerous channel or trolling in large, potentially nauseating waves didn't worry them, so we loaded their coolers full of food and off we went.

We pulled out of the slip and idled down the narrow aisle between boats. Clearing the last dock, I lightly pressed down on the throttle and made a hard left turn into the short channel. Passing the gas dock, I hammered the throttle and the boat jumped up onto plane and we roared through the breakers. The next 20 seconds was a bit like downhill skiing, tobogganing, riding a rollercoaster and surfing rolled into one great rush!

After clearing the channel we jumped from wave top to wave top and I'll never forget what happened next. I took my hat off . . . and one of my clients from Iowa looked at me, his jaw dropped and his eyes about popped out of his head. Then he calmly said, "Oh my God, Ethel! What have we gotten ourselves into?" He wasn't talking about the waves or the boat ride through the channel. He was talking about my haircut. If you were to judge me by my appearance that summer, you would have thought I belonged in a punk band or in front of a parole board—certainly not on a fishing boat. That summer I learned to keep my hat on until we were well offshore.

I may have been a bit rough around the edges when I began chartering, but I was absolutely crazy about fishing and water. I truly think I was more at home on the water than on dry land. My fishing techniques were primitive, but very productive in the burgeoning Lake

Michigan salmon and trout fishery. Being young and new to the business, my tackle was limited and my boat's electronics were, how should I say, pretty crummy. I had a marine radio and an old Vexilar paper graph that seemed to work when it felt like, which wasn't very often. Since I wasn't very good at fixing things I developed the attitude that anglers who depended on gadgets and gizmos to catch fish were somehow weaker than those who could *read* the water and catch fish by pure gut instinct.

The foundation of my charter business was built on the Mako but after two seasons I upgraded to a 27-foot Sportcraft. This boat was outfitted with the latest technology, which included an amber screen sonar, an autopilot and a Loran C. Way back then (am I really that old?) GPS was not available but Loran would triangulate your position from land-based radio signals. Like many things in my life at the time, the Loran didn't work, but it sure looked impressive mounted on the dash! After a few years I finally figured out it needed a special antennae adaptation, but hey, I was never good at fixing things. I just went fishing without Loran to help ascertain where I was.

If you've ever chased salmon on big water, you know that being in the right spot at the right time is tantamount to success. This is especially true on Lake Michigan, an enormous inland sea that's 307 miles long and as much as 118 miles wide. The region's rapidly changing weather patterns, the lake's shifting currents and tightly spaced, steep waves further complicate an angler's task. Without any electronics to interpret this challenging environment I refined my observational skills at an early age. Experience trained me to note subtle changes in the water texture, currents, weather, bottom topography and fish behavior.

Whether navigating or staying with an active school of fish I relied on line of sight. I got really good at reading the angles of landmarks and interpreting my position based on my intimate knowledge of bottom topography. I learned to time my trolling passes (for example, a 30-minute troll to the north, and 35 minutes back south), estimate the speed of the current based on wind velocity, the angle of my lines in the water and the sound (rpm's) of my engine. Stone age fishing! In my mind I always knew where I was. At least I convinced myself and my customers that I knew. But the truth is, sometimes I was farther off course than I ever imagined.

My friend and fellow captain, Arnie Arredondo, was too eager to point that out. He knew my limited selection of electronics didn't work. When sharing information on the water he learned to ask, "Dan, where do you *think* you are?" I was always quite sure of my location, but over time, he showed me that my "dead reckoning" wasn't always accurate. In fact, one foggy day I was certain I was only a 20-minute run from the harbor. When it took me close to an hour to get back to port, I realized I was way off-course. Back then, when I lost sight of shore, I had nothing to gauge my position by, other than my instincts.

It's easy to lose our way. On the water, heavy seas and fog can confuse us. Ashore, a busy schedule at work or home, a few bad choices, an addiction or a broken relationship can knock us off course. When fishing, I was never afraid to ask for help from friends like Arnie. When on land, I was sure I knew it all, rarely asking for help from anyone and not realizing just how far off course I was. After all, the world is filled with false landmarks. How about you? When you're fishing, do you seek other anglers' advice on the hot lure, right depth and best location to catch the most fish? We're so eager to sharpen our angling abilities and learn the latest techniques! What about life? Do you ask for assistance when the rest of your life doesn't seem to add up?

When it comes to navigating our daily challenges and major life hurdles men have a hard time asking for help. Technology and cultural trends encourage each of us to go through life like a *lone wolf.* Like a boat venturing out to sea during storm warnings, a lone wolf is one bad decision away from disaster when he sails through life solo.

That's exactly where the enemy wants a man to be—alone and cut off from other believers. But, God also provides some valuable resources to help you connect with other brothers in Christ and to keep you from drifting off course. Think of it as "God's Tackle Box." Open it to find the friends, divinely appointed experiences and other "tools" that will lead you through a turbulent culture. (We will explore this in "One More Cast.")

Staying the Course

Before we go any further I should also mention that some of you, like me, might have internalized some beliefs and values that are in total conflict with who God really is. You'll need to let Jesus rebuild you, HIS way, according to HIS blueprint, one day at a time, from the inside out. This will take time and the tips offered in *One More Cast* will point you in the right direction.

One of the ways God rebuilds you is by sending the Holy Spirit to live in you.

In John 16, Jesus was preparing the disciples for his departure. I'm guessing that some of them were frightened and others may not have had a clue what he was talking about. But Jesus encouraged them and said, "If I do not go away, the Helper will not come to you. But if I go, I will send him to you" (John 16:7). The role of the Spirit is to *help* us, and he does it in a number of ways.

The Spirit is our internal compass. He speaks through our conscience and convicts us of our sin. He empowers us and gives us the energy to live a Godly life and serve others. When we stumble, the Spirit purifies us and assures us of our salvation. When you find yourself in a difficult or compromising situation, it is the Spirit that reminds you of God's Word.

The Spirit lives in all believers. As you grow, ask the Spirit to re-align your will with God's will. Seek the Spirit's leadership in your life and learn to recognize his voice. Some folks get confused here and are willing to listen to anything that pops into their head. The best way to know his voice is by reading your Bible. The Bible is a living book and the Spirit brings the text to life and helps you to live it out. The Helper never contradicts the teaching of the Bible but will help you understand it and will lead you to the truth.

Ready, Fire, Aim!

If you were sitting on my boat and asked me, "Dan, how can I become a better fisherman?" I would begin with the basics. When I teach fishing seminars I always build upon four key principles. How to find fish, analyze the conditions, choose the best lure (bait) and presentation. Everything is built on these! Great anglers master these crucial fundamentals and learn how to execute them in all situations.

If you were in my boat (or anywhere else) and asked me, "Dan, how do I grow in faith?" I would start with the basics, too. God is real and he loves you enough to forgive your sins. Your faith is a relationship with Jesus Christ. The Bible is accurate and trustworthy. Your identity is found in Christ alone and he will give you the power to grow.

The foundation of your relationship is an authentic faith in Jesus. My buddy Kurt calls it the "faith principle." This core truth will bring clarity to your vision and breathe life into your soul. And who better to teach us than Peter.

Peter was rather impulsive. He was passionate and zealous, but not always wise. "Ready, fire, aim!" was his motto. His enthusiasm to tackle a problem got him into trouble on more than one occasion. But Jesus was extremely patient with him, and this man who used to live like a heat seeking missile wound up challenging us to be clear about our faith, and to grow up in Christ.

The key lesson that Jesus taught Peter was to trust him, and what better place to teach him than on a stormy lake? Late one night during the fourth watch (between 3:00 and 6:00 a.m.) the disciples were sailing across the Sea of Galilee. A storm with a strong headwind had slowed their progress and threatened to sink them. I wonder if the boat was taking on water and someone was bailing in the stern? As they battled the waves, Jesus came to them, strolling across the water! You and I have seen a lot of special effects, so when we read this Bible passage, a guy walking on water doesn't exactly chill us to our marrow. But put yourself in the place of these disciples 2,000 years ago. They see a man walking on water and it terrifies them! Some even thought it was a ghost! But Jesus called out to them and said, "Do not be afraid." Peter, always ready for action, said, "Lord, if it's you, tell me to come to you on the water" (Matthew 14:28 NIV). Jesus replied, "Come."

Peter then did the unthinkable; he stepped across the gunnels of his boat. He got out of the boat and . . . he started walking on the water, too! But suddenly, Peter shifted his focus from Jesus to the wind in his face and the large waves beneath his feet. Fear overwhelmed him and he began to sink. Like so many of us he cried out to Jesus. "Immediately Jesus reached out his hand and caught him. 'You of little faith,' he said, 'why did you doubt" (Matthew 14:31 NIV)?

In a situation tailor-made for Peter, Jesus was teaching his hard-headed disciple to trust him. And not just so Peter could walk on water. Jesus taught Peter to trust him in every situation, with every possession, with every relationship and with every fear—no matter the circumstances or Peter's emotional state.

Peter didn't learn this lesson overnight. Truth is, he was a lot like us. He didn't always make the best choice, like the time he sliced a guy's ear off with a sword (we'll save that story for another book). But on the raging waters, Jesus taught Peter the most valuable lesson—to trust Jesus no matter how fierce the wind was blowing or how unthinkable the task. When Peter trusted Jesus, he saw God do supernatural work in his life. When Peter lost his focus, he sank.

It's the same for us. Jesus wants us to trust him. He wants us to focus on him, regardless of our feelings, circumstances or the latest cultural trend. Our world is moving faster than ever, and it's easy to be consumed by our hectic schedules and the demands of life. Jesus doesn't want us to be distracted by the wind or waves, the loss of a job, a broken relationship, a dwindling savings account or a difficult health challenge. He wants us to focus on him. The foundation of every decision, of every act of obedience and repentance, of our love for God and neighbors is all anchored by our confidence in Jesus. When you trust Jesus with your life, work, family, health, savings, sins, recreation, abilities, everything; there is no telling what God will do in your life. Who knows, you may even find yourself walking on water!

Hang on for the Ride

As a charter captain, I get to go fishing—a lot! While calm water and sunny skies make life easier on the deck of a boat, truth is, I love the challenge of fishing in rough water. There is something magical about locating fish and running a spread of lines in big waves that makes me come to life. Over time, rough water has tested my angling ability, and made me a better angler.

Just like Peter's struggle with faith in the storm, your faith will be tested. Don't worry, for just as rough water sharpens our angling ability, God uses the trials of life to mold you into a Godly man. One of Peter's friends, Paul, can teach us much about living in a sinful world. I think you would like him. Paul's commitment to spreading the gospel led him on three journeys. He survived three shipwrecks in the Mediterranean Sea, was bitten by a deadly snake, chased by an angry mob, stoned (nearly to death) and eventually wound up in a Roman prison. How fitting that he should tell us to *work out our salvation* (Philippians 2:12).

This doesn't mean we earn salvation. I want to be clear about this. You cannot earn it. Salvation is a gift. But your relationship with Jesus is meant to touch every corner of your life. It is a relationship that is alive and active. It's more than just talking about nice Christian things and going to church on Sunday mornings. It's more than buying a Bible and putting it on your shelf. It is the blending of your life with your faith in Jesus. You live it out through the events, relationships and challenges of your life. *Working out your salvation* is a process that leads you closer to God. It's not a daily checklist, nor is it a list of rules and regulations. When you seek him, you will experience deeper amazement and gain a greater sense of wonder about who God is. When you are right with God, obedience becomes a reflection of your relationship with him.

As you *work out your salvation*, it will transform you and those around you. Think of an athlete. When an athlete begins playing a sport the first things the coach teaches him are the fundamentals. When my son Ethan first started playing soccer, we practiced passing and dribbling skills in the backyard. After a few days, he thought he was ready for action. But after a couple games, he realized that he needed to practice even the most basic skills to become a better soccer player.

Core fundamentals are the foundation of success. Through training, an athlete perfects his skills. Vigorous exercise builds up his muscles and increases his endurance. When he enters the big game, he is prepared for action. He doesn't choke under pressure but has the strength, stamina and talent to compete—and win. Truly great athletes do one other thing; they raise the level of the players around them.

When you exercise your faith, you prepare yourself (heart, mind and body) for action. You submit to the teaching of the Word and build upon God's core truths. You allow God to shape your inner character. You trust God through difficult situations and persevere even when strong headwinds are blowing. Whether you are tested by storm-force winds or blessed with calm waters, you will be ready for action.

Some days, though, "working out" our salvation is just hard work! We don't always *feel* like a new person and some of our old habits and sins haunt us. My buddy Jim Klausing discovered the tension of living in a fallen world. I think many of us can relate to Jim's struggles.

Jim is an avid tournament fisherman and recently retired firefighter. After surrendering his life to Christ, Jim still struggled with his sins and emotions. When things got tense during tournaments he didn't always choose the best words. At the fire station his old lifestyle would taunt him and he found himself thinking unhealthy thoughts. His friends and co-workers knew he was a Christ follower and they watched him more closely than ever. If Jim made a mistake, the guys were quick to jump on him.

Jim loved the Lord and was troubled by his sins. (That's the Holy Spirit working in Jim's heart!) At times he felt like giving up. But he learned that God doesn't give up on us. "He who began a good work in you will bring it to completion at the day of Jesus Christ" (Philippians 1:6). Jim is a work in progress and, with Jesus' help, he is learning to control and channel his emotions and passions. Jim learned that the first step to overcoming sin is to confess it to God, "If we confess our sins, He is faithful and just to forgive us our sins and to cleanse us from all unrighteousness" (1 John 1:9).

Being a Christ follower is a life long commitment that unfolds over the course of our lives. Like Jim, as we grow, Christ empowers us to break away from old habits. Sinful patterns can be hard to shake, but with Jesus' help, we can overcome them, "I can do all things through him who strengthens me" (Philippians 4:13).

Poisonous Doubt

As you start your life as a Christian, or even if you've been a Jesus follower for many years, you will no doubt run into an old adversary many believers face: doubt. When doubt creeps into your mind, it can destroy you from the inside out. On more than one occasion I've asked myself, "God are you really there? Do you still care about me?" This usually happens during a storm, and like Peter, Jesus wants to teach you to trust him. During moments like these you need to remember that Jesus' words are true and that, "He will never leave you or forsake you" (Hebrews 13:5). Remember, your new life in Christ is a process, and that each one of us is a work in progress. Even though you will stumble, the trajectory of your growth will be, overall, an upward curve.

Upgrade Your Life

Many years ago I upgraded to a 27-foot Sportcraft. She had many advanced features which would make me a better angler; but only if I learned how to use them. Unfortunately, back then, I had a chip on my shoulder and didn't think I needed the upgrades. How could this new boat and electronics make me a better fisherman? Plus, the thought of step-by-step installation and learning how to use these things was overwhelming. So, I stubbornly clung to some of my old fishing habits and didn't even take the time to set up the new Loran navigation system—I was always in such a hurry to fish! After all, I always thought I knew where I was, even when I didn't.

It took me years to embrace the technology on my new boat but when I did, I was catching more fish than ever before. When you become a Christian, make use of the spiritual, physical and eternal upgrades God has for you. Your identity is found in Christ and he calls you to turn from a sinful life and to follow him. His upgrades will restore your soul and guide you. They will protect you from the storms of life and help you chart an eternal course.

God has so much in store for you, and it begins on this side of eternity. Eternal life begins the moment you are rescued! You see, Jesus isn't calling us to a place; he's calling us to a life, "So, whoever has the Son, has life; whoever rejects the Son, rejects life" (1 John 5:12 MSG). When you seek him with your whole heart he will strengthen you and give you a level of peace and understanding that is as wide and as deep as the oceans.

When you allow Jesus to take the helm, your life is transformed into a journey of discovery. Just as a newborn moves from milk to solid food, a Christ follower grows up in his faith. In other words, your faith, your life, is a work in progress. We should no longer act like children. "God wants us to grow up, to know the whole truth and tell it in love—like Christ in everything. We take our lead from Christ, who is the source of everything we do. He keeps us in step with each other. His very breath and blood flow through us, nourishing us so that we will grow up healthy in God, robust in love" (Ephesians 4:15-16 MSG).

Before we part company, let's make *one more cast* and look inside God's Tackle Box. It took me years to open my tackle box. I hope you don't make the same mistake.

A truly good book teaches me better than to read it;
I must soon lay it down, and commence living on its hint;
what I began by reading, I must finish by acting.
—HENRY DAVID THOREAU

One More Cast

I 'll never forget the trip Dad and I took to Basswood Lake in Minnesota when I was a youngster. The week before we departed, I was so excited that I couldn't think of anything else. I read everything I could get my hands on so I would know how to catch the smallmouth, walleye and northern pike that were up there waiting for us! We spent hours preparing our rods and reels and packing our tackle box. Extra line, hooks and sinkers, plus an assortment of our favorite Mepps spinners and Rapala floating minnows were neatly organized for the adventure ahead. We would be camping in a remote region accessible only by boat, so the last thing we wanted was to be caught without the right gear or lures.

This may seem like a silly question, but would you set out on a week-long fishing trip to a remote lake loaded with fish and not take any tackle? Would you just show up at the lake, with only the clothes on your back and expect to catch fish? As fishermen, we all know that having a game plan, using the right tackle, and having a clear understanding of the water and fish makes us better anglers. Is life any different than a fishing trip? Having clarity about God, your neighbor and yourself, plus using God's resources can be a huge help to you as you navigate the challenges of living in a fallen world.

I have enjoyed sharing parts of my journey with you and introducing you to Simon Peter, and would like to offer you a few final tips until we meet again. God has a spiritual tackle box with your name on it. It is filled with tools, resources and divinely appointed experiences that will help you grow into the man he designed you to be. These seven essential resources will encourage you and strengthen you in your journey. Extra line, an assortment of lures, terminal tackle, bait, maps, a GPS and compass can all help our angling success. Get in the habit of using the stuff in God's tackle box. It will help you to grow and live courageously and free.

GOD'S TACKLE BOX

Your Compass: The Holy Spirit

Have you ever hiked across a heavily forested valley? It's easy to lose your way when thick undergrowth or a steep ridge or ravine forces you off track. A compass will guide you back on course. A compass always points to true north. When you follow Jesus, God places an internal compass—the Holy Spirit—inside you. The Spirit leads you and guides you, helping you to grow in love, joy, peace, patience, kindness, goodness, faithfulness, gentleness, and self control. He often speaks through your conscience, never contradicting what God wrote in the Bible, and even helping you remember encouraging verses when you need help with doubts or temptations. "The Spirit will teach you all things and bring to your remembrance all that I have said" (John 14:26).

A Map: The Bible

Growing up, my family would head north to Wisconsin's Manitowish Waters or the Eagle River Chain of Lakes for a week or two in August.

It was a vacation of endless pine trees, always a trip to Paul Bunyan's famous logging restaurant and water skiing—and, of course, fishing with my dad! Before the first cast ever hit the water we would study topographical maps of the lakes. We wanted to familiarize ourselves with the drop-offs, sunken islands, weed beds and any structure that might hold fish. Before we ever left the dock, we had a plan!

Maps and charts make us better anglers. The more we study them, the greater our understanding of a lake and its fish. They also protect us from danger as they reveal sandbars, sunken timber, reefs, wrecks and other obstacles that can damage our boats, motors and tackle.

God has given us the Holy Bible as a map to guide us and protect us. Through narrative, poetry and history, God's Word tells us God's story and lets us realize how our story fits into his story. Sadly, many think that the Bible is merely a big stick intended to keep them from living large, a book written to put the damper on any party. Nothing could be further from the truth!

The Bible is God's living Word. It gives life, explains life, protects life and enables you to share life with others. At its core, the Bible helps us understand who God is, and who we are. God's Word nourishes our souls and teaches us how to live. On a more sober note, it also warns us of danger that can sink us if we make poor choices.

The Bible is trustworthy and reliable. Take the time to learn and understand God's Word. Get in the habit of reading the Bible every day. In *The Ragamuffin Gospel*, Brennan Manning tells us that we must "sit still in the presence of the living word." As you read the Bible ask God to help you understand it in your heart as well as in your head. Ask him to help you learn to apply it to your life.

Communication: Prayer

Good communication leads to success at work, home or on the water. One day I was trolling in 120 feet of water and, to be honest, was running out of stories to tell my clients. In other words, we weren't catching any fish! I assumed the other charter boats were struggling but unexpectedly my buddy Bob phoned me to let me know the steelhead and kings were *biting the props off,* out just beyond 200 feet of water. He didn't even have time to tell me what the fish were hitting. He just said, "Get out here!" Once we crossed into deeper water, *wham!* It was like Christmas morning and New Years Eve rolled into one explosive moment. We couldn't keep the fish off our lines! Because Bob and I were in the habit of talking and sharing information, a very slow charter turned into a great success.

As a Christ follower, you have a direct line to God through prayer. The Bible tells us that we can call on God anytime, day or night. Paul tells us to *pray continually.* Best of all, we can talk to God about anything. Maybe it's a fear of the unknown, a health problem, a temptation that keeps getting the best of you, a relationship that is suffering, or a friend who needs help—you name it—you can bring anything to him. Don't talk to God just when you want something or have problems. Tell God how thankful you are for the chance to live in his world. Thank him for unexpected blessings and good days. A healthy praise habit is good for your soul.

Prayer is really an ongoing, two-way conversation between you and God that will draw you closer to him. A healthy prayer habit means you learn to be still, to meditate on God's Word and to *listen.* Listen to him. Weave prayer and Scripture reading together. God speaks to us through his written Word, the Bible. When you encounter storms in life, a healthy prayer habit will make the big waves seem smaller. Consistent prayer brings peace, clarity, direction and yes, the occasional miracle into your life.

GPS: Jesus Christ

When I first started guiding, it was truly me against the fish! Without electronics, my fish-finding instincts had to be razor sharp. Today, we fishermen rely on GPS (yes, I now have a functioning GPS unit on my boat) for navigating and to pinpoint our location with precise accuracy. If you've ever navigated across open water when fog and heavy rain is making it hard to see and large waves are pushing you off course, you know how a GPS can help lead you to your final destination.

When we follow Jesus Christ, he is our GPS. He tells us where we are going and how to get there. He is the standard by which we can measure our thoughts and actions. When Jesus walked the dusty roads of primitive Palestine, he showed us how to live, and he did it perfectly. When our internal compass, the Holy Spirit, nudges us about something, we can check our behavior in light of how Jesus lived and acted. When we get lost he will, just like a GPS signal, lead us back on course. You can trust me on this topic—I know a lot about getting lost.

Some of you may be thinking that Jesus will give you more than you can handle. Let me assure you, Jesus is not an overbearing taskmaster. He tells us, "I won't lay anything heavy or ill-fitting on you. Keep company with me and you'll learn to live freely and lightly" (Matthew 11:29,30 MSG). He knows exactly what you can and cannot handle. When you set your life coordinates on Jesus, he will recalibrate your heart. He will lead you through the challenges and temptations of life and bring you securely to your final destination with him.

Spiritual Sunglasses: Christian Brothers

I have fished around the world but my favorite destination is Florida. As our annual Thanksgiving trip to my parents' home there approaches, I often find myself daydreaming about drifting my favorite flats or running the beaches looking for schools of feeding fish. On the flats or in shallow bays a good pair of sunglasses is as important as the tackle. Sunglasses protect our eyes, eliminate glare and help us to peer into the water and find fish. Without our shades we get worn out from the glare of the blistering sun and we cannot see clearly.

Likewise, Christian friends protect us from the glare and glitter of this ungodly world and help us to see clearly. If you are a Christ follower, don't attempt life's journey alone. Being a lone wolf makes life a lot more difficult and a whole lot less fun. Prayerfully, seek out a friend or two who can be your companion as you take on life's challenges. Better yet, seek out a spiritual coach or mentor who can walk beside you. Just as a fishing guide can dial you into a hot bite, a mentor can help lead you into a rich and rewarding life. Share your frustrations, sorrows, temptations, joys and victories. When faced with tough choices or temptation, a strong, reliable friend can help you make the right choice. I have several friends (pairs of sunglasses) I view difficult situations through. I seek their advice before I act. I also ask them to keep difficult situations in prayer. Good brothers encourage and sharpen us. Together, we are stronger.

Hope: God's Promise

I've never met a fisherman who wasn't filled with hope. After all, fishermen have eyes of faith. They believe that they will be able to catch what is unseen below the water's surface. From first light on the water to the last cast, we are filled with hope at what might be. We are filled with the hope that we will catch a fish and that the next fish will be bigger, the next memory sweeter, the next sunrise brighter. Hope is a shield that protects us when we encounter setbacks. Maybe you've lost a big fish in the final hour of a tournament? Hope keeps us from losing faith and despairing. Hope pushes us to finish despite the setbacks. Hope inspires us to persevere.

Applying our faith to fishing creates hope on the water. It inspires confidence in us. We don't get distracted by the other guy's boat or tackle. We don't give up on the techniques that we know will produce fish. When we apply hope to fishing, we succeed. In life, our hope is now a God-centered confidence. We are confident in God's Word and we don't give up on his promises, or his people. When facing difficulties, we know that God is in control. Nothing happens by accident. When we look beyond the horizon of our lives and acknowledge the unseen parts, "We have our hope set on the living God" (1 Timothy 4:10).

Spiritual Teamwork: Community

Authentic Christianity is a team sport. Salvation is not a ticket to a game where you grab a large soda and popcorn and head up into the bleachers to watch the pastor do all the work. When Jesus rescues you, you become a member of a team.

When I troll for salmon and trout I typically run a 12-line spread. I use a combination of delivery devices (downriggers, diver disks, planer boards, etc.) to reach the target depth and to spread lines out to the side. I also use a variety of different lines including mono, braided line, leadcore and wire line. When it comes to lure selection, I have thousands of lures from which to choose. If the fish are aggressive, I will use flashers and flies. If stealth is called for, I put out clean spoons with fluorocarbon leaders. If facing ultra-cold water, then crankbaits may join the team. I begin each day with a combination of lines and lures.

As the day unfolds, I make adjustments to my spread. I don't just set lines and sit down. I observe my environment and factor in a variety of variables including light intensity, weather, current and fish temperament. I may raise baits up in the water column, or drop them deeper. I tweak my trolling speed and angle over the bottom as I weave a variety of lures and delivery devices into a complete spread. My goal is to attract maximum numbers of fish into my spread and to trigger strikes. When I work my gear and lures as a team, I catch more fish.

A Christ follower is a member of a bigger team, moving together toward larger goals: to be God's ambassadors to the world, to build each other up in the faith and to worship God through our lives. Every member of the team is uniquely created and each has a vital role to play. In fact, Paul uses a great analogy in 1 Corinthians 12 about how our bodies have lots of parts, and how each part—whether the foot, the hand, the eye or the nose—is important. What is your role? Seek out an authentic community of Christ followers who are passionately engaging with God. Join them. Find a good, Bible-believing church where you can plug in. Let me caution you. Churches are jam-packed with broken, sinful people. As you look for a home church and a community, keep your focus on Jesus, not the shortcomings of others.

Being a Christian, a Christ follower, is much more than a Sunday morning trip to the local church. It is more than an intellectual decision, such as *believing in* gravity or that the Chicago Cubs will ever win a World Series. *Being* a Christian is something you do every day, sort of like breathing. It is an active, intentional engaging of your entire being that encompasses every facet of your life. Your thoughts and actions reflect your relationship with God, and over time you grow and become the man God designed you to be.

> *Your life is a journey you must travel with*
> *a deep consciousness of God.*
>
> —THE APOSTLE PETER

Acknowledgments

This book is the culmination of many experiences, friendships and difficult challenges. The idea for the book was planted back in 2002 when my friend Bob Roberts took a book off the shelf and tossed it at me and said, "Hey Keating, why don't you write a book like this, but from a fisherman's perspective." Well, I chewed on that thought and after moving from Illinois to Colorado, and back to Illinois, the book has finally come to fruition.

Were it not for God's grace, and the help and prayers of many faithful friends, I could not have written this book. Mom and Dad, thank you for allowing my angling passions to grow at an early age! To my beloved wife Mary, thank you for your patience and support as I've pondered this work. To our four indescribable children, Rebecca, Ethan, Kate and Chloë, your encouragement and prayers are an inspiration.

We have seen God's hand direct this project from the beginning and want to thank Greg and Karen Magee for their generous support, and timely encouragement in helping to make this book a reality. I've had a great deal of help from many faithful friends. Thank you John Lillyman, John Mulder, Jim Klausing, Paul Blue, Dave Anderson, Chris Mitchell, Steve Laubenstein and Barb Kelley for reading and commenting on the many, many early drafts. You guys are a part of this book! I would especially like to thank my friend Kurt Loosenort, who, in the bottom of the ninth, stepped in and made some huge contributions. Kurt, you are a natural editor!

Thank you to Angie for taking on this *little fish* in spite of working with all the *big fish*. Mary and I still wonder what made you say yes when we came to you with the first book. But we're glad you did, you're a pleasure to work with. You always go beyond the extra mile. Thank you Josh for sharing your creativity with us. Not only was it great working with you again, but we even got a chance to fish together, and will again! Jennifer, you were an unexpected blessing in extra innings. Thank you for making this book better.

Finally, I want to thank my two editors, Bob Roberts and Dave Mull. I could not have done this without your faithful and skillful assistance. Thank you for having a sense of humor as you've gently encouraged my writing. Bob, you've put many long hours into this project and have added greatly to the structure of this book. Dave, your help crafting this manuscript and your encouragement with the *Angling Life* column has inspired me and made me a stronger writer. You have brought much color to this book.

This is the first leg of, Lord willing, a three book series exploring the connection between our love of fishing, the outdoors and our faith in God.

Thirty Waypoints to Anchor Your Life

Many fishermen keep a logbook of their favorite hot spots. When anglers look at a new lake they often don't know where to make their first cast. Likewise, my friend Kurt Loosenort knows many don't know where to make their first cast into the Word of God. He has graciously offered to share his personal *logbook*. These foundational verses will guide you to a deeper and more powerful relationship with God. Take one waypoint and corresponding verse a day and contemplate its meaning. Allow the words to sink into your heart and transform your mind and your life.

Week One:
God's Revelation of Himself

Day 1: Creation (Psalm 19).

Day 2: God's Word is reliable (2 Timothy 3: 16,17 and Hebrews 4:12).

Day 3: Fulfilled prophecy (2 Peter 1:20-21).

Day 4: Jesus' Claims (John 14:6).

Day 5: Jesus' resurrection (1 Corinthians 15:3-6).

Day 6: Who is like God (Isaiah 40:25)?

Day 7: Jesus encouraged his disciples to question his identity (Matthew 16:13-16).

Week Two:
God Invites Us to Begin a Relationship with Him

Day 1:   God loves people and wants us to engage in a relationship
with Him (John 3:16).

Day 2:   Sin separates us from God. When we reject Jesus Christ, we
will not see (eternal) life (John 3:36).

Day 3:   When we receive Jesus, we become a child of God and are
given a new identity and a new birth (John 1:12 and John 3:3).

Day 4:   When we receive Jesus, he promises never to abandon us
(John 6:35-37).

Day 5:   Jesus promises that no one can take us out of his hand
(John 10:27-29).

Day 6:   Nothing can separate us from his love (Romans 8:38-39).

Day 7:   He wants us to know that we have eternal life because we
have Christ (1 John 5:11-13).

Week Three:
God Wants Us to Grow in Our Relationship with Him

Day 1:   God is at work in us, giving us the desire and power to live
according to his purpose (Philippians 2:13).

Day 2:   Jesus lives through our lives, as we trust him (Galatians 2:20).

Day 3:   Confessing our sins, being cleansed of our guilt, free from
slavery to sin (1 John 1:9).

Day 4:   We are empowered by the Spirit living in us and through us
(Galatians 5:16-26, Ephesians 5:18).

Day 5:   Being confident in, guided by and obedient to his reliable
word (2 Timothy 3:16-17).

Day 6: Healthy teamwork with other believers and strong community (church) for prayer, strengthening, coaching and equipping (Acts 2:42).

Day 7: When we obey his commands, he reveals himself to us (John 14:21).

Week Four:
Designed to Make an Impact—We Grow Best When We Help Others Know God and Grow in Him

Day 1: When we follow Christ, he equips us to bring others into a relationship with him (Matthew 4:19).

Day 2: We have been commanded to, "Be prepared to share the good news clearly, with gentleness and respect" (1 Peter 3:15).

Day 3: God gives us power to be his witness, here, and around the world (Acts 1:8).

Day 4: We have been called to bear fruit for God and to lead others to new life (John 15:4-5).

Day 5: We have been commanded to "make disciples," to equip others to follow him (Matthew 28:18-20).

Day 6: Share what you learn about God with others (2 Timothy 2:2).

Day 7: Being a Christ follower is a team sport. Grow with others (Ephesians 4:12,16).

Rough Water Beacons

Trust God even when life doesn't make sense (Proverbs 3:5-6).
Power and strength for the journey (Ephesians 3:16-20).

Recommended Books and Music

Books

More Than a Carpenter by Josh McDowell and Sean McDowell, Living Books.

The Life You've Always Wanted by John Ortberg, Zondervan Publishers.

Wild at Heart: Discover the Secret of a Man's Soul by John Eldredge, Thomas Nelson.

Basic Christianity by John Stott and Rick Warren, IVP Books.

Mere Christianity by C.S. Lewis, Harper San Francisco.

The Barbarian Way: Unleash the Untamed Faith Within by Erwin Raphael McManus, Thomas Nelson.

The Cross of Christ by John Stott, IVP Books.

The Purpose-Driven Life: What on Earth Am I Here For? by Rick Warren, Zondervan.

A Look at Life from a Deer Stand by Steve Chapman, Harvest House Publishers.

10 Things I Want My Son to Know: Getting Him Ready for Life by Steve Chapman, Harvest House Publishers.

Has Christianity Failed You? by Ravi Zacharias, Zondervan.

Jesus Among Other Gods: The Absolute Claims of the Christian Message by Ravi Zacharias, W Publishing Group.

Recapture the Wonder: Experiencing God's Amazing Promise of Childlike Joy by Ravi Zacharias, Integrity Publishers.

Crazy Love by Francis Chan, David C. Cook.

Wild Men, Wild Alaska: Finding What Lies Beyond the Limits by Rocky McElveen, Thomas Nelson.

Why Sin Matters: The Surprising Relationship Between Our Sin and God's Grace by Mark R. McMinn, Tyndale House Publishers.

The Ragamuffin Gospel by Brennan Manning, Multnomah Books.

Music

Aaron Schust: *Whispered and Shouted*

Caedemon's Call: *Back Home*

Casting Crowns: *Casting Crowns, The Altar and the Door, Lifesong*

David Crowder Band: *Illuminate*

Jars of Clay: *Jars of Clay*

Jeremy Camp: *Speaking Louder Than Before*

Mark Tedder: *Pilgrims Journey, Restore, The Door*

Matthew West: *Something to Say*

Mercy Me: *Almost There, Undone, Coming Up to Breathe*

Newsboys: *Devotion, Step Up To The Microphone, Shine: The Hits*

Sanctus Real: *Fight the Tide*

Skillet: *Awake*

Steven Curtis Chapman: *Greatest Hits*

Switchfoot: *Dare You to Move*

Third Day: *Revelation*

About the Author

Captain Dan Keating is author of *Keating on Kings: Great Lakes Chinook Tactics Way Beyond the Basics,* often referred to as the "bible" of salmon fishing books. He has also produced two DVDs capturing the essence and techniques of locating and catching salmon and trout. He is also coauthor of *Great Lakes Salmon and Trout Fishing: The Complete Troller's Guide.* Captain Dan is a full time fishing guide operating on the waters of Lake Michigan. He is a light tackle specialist who has built his reputation on his ability to find and catch fish when others can't.

In the off-season, Dan teaches highly informative fishing clinics across the Great Lakes region. He also speaks at churches and outreach events. Like this book, Dan blends fishing, the challenges of life, his testimony and the gospel message into an exciting format that can be geared toward outreach or discipleship. When not on the water he enjoys spending time with his wife, Mary, and their four children, gardening, hiking in the mountains of Colorado and fishing for snook (or anything with fins) out the back door of his parents' home in Florida. Dan and Mary have had many exciting adventures fishing off the beaten path in remote locations around the world.

Let us know what you think of this book or email us any questions you have at anglinglife@gmail.com.

To learn more about having Dan speak at your church, men's events or fishing clinic; or for more information about his books and fishing charters visit www.anglinglife.net or www.bluehorizonsportfishing.net to learn more.